EDWARDIAN HATS:

The Art of Millinery (1909)

BY MME. ANNA BEN-YUSUF

Enlarged & Edited by R.L. Shep

Additional Illustrations from
Correct Dress: Fall & Winter 1908-9
Franklin Simon & Co., New York

R.L. Shep
Mendocino

Copyright ©1992 by R.L. Shep

This work contains the complete original *The Art of Millinery* of 1909 and illustrations from the Franklin Simon & Co., Fall & Winter 1908-9 catalogue: *Correct Dress*.

ISBN 0-914046-15-2

Library of Congress #92-093330

Printed in the United States of America.

Published by:
R.L. Shep
Box 668
Mendocino, CA 95460

Library of Congress Cataloging-in-Publication Data

Ben-Yûsuf, Anna.
    Edwardian hats : the art of millinery (1909) / by Anna Ben-Yusuf ;
  enlarged & edited by R.L. Shep.
        p.   cm.
    Rev. ed. of: The art of millinery. 1909.
    ISBN 0-914046-15-2 (pbk.) : $24.95
    1. Millinery.   I. Shep. R. L., 1933-   . II. Ben-Yûsuf, Anna.
  Art of millinery. III. Title.
  TT655.B5   1992
  646.5'04--dc20
                                                        92-93330
                                                            CIP

CONTENTS

NOTES

When you look at illustrations of the Edwardian Era you are at once drawn to the fact that everyone wears hats. Men wore hats, and they were nice, but there is no doubt that they were fairly plain. Children wore hats a good part of the time too. But it is with women's hats that the milliner's art reached its height.

There are a number of reasons why women's hats were so large and so extravagant. Part of this has to do with line and silhouette, and part of it has to do with the way women were wearing their hair. The pompadour lent itself to wearing large hats well forward on the head.

wonderful and expressive is due to the way women thought of themselves. They were coming out from under the strictness of the Victorian Era and, although their clothes were changing, they were changing slowly right up through the first World War. But hats changed rapidly, and it was a way that a woman could really express herself.

The milliner was in great demand and was represented by several trade magazines including the *Millinery Trade Review*, for which the author wrote. She had a well grounded career in Paris and London and finally in New York where she taught at Pratt Institute. She also wrote the millinery section of Clara Laughton's *The Complete Dressmaker* in 1907.

This book is particularly valuable because it was written by a leading milliner and teacher of the times. In this way we can see the methods that were used at that time to produce the hats of the period. She stresses that it is necessary to have a knowledge of how hats are made even if you are only a designer and do not intend to do the work yourself. It is only through this knowledge that you will be able to design it properly.

In order to give you a broader look at some of the hats of the times, we have added a number of illustrations from a good New York mail order house catalogue. The hats shown here, and in the body of the book, are of good quality and fairly middle of the road in terms of style.

ADDITIONAL ILLUSTRATIONS

Fifth Avenue, New York.

76.   78.   80.

WOMEN'S DRESSY TAILORED SUITS.
Sizes 32 to 44.

No. 76. Stylish Tailored Suit, of self striped broadcloth, in navy, olive or stone green, tobacco brown or black, also of plain broadcloth, in catawba, wistaria, taupe, stone, navy, brown or black, coat trimmed front and back with fancy black silk braid, buttons, revers and facing of black satin, fastened with cord ornaments, coat lined with heavy striped silk and interlined, princess skirt 45.00

No. 78. Handsome Velvet Suit, in smoke, amethyst, green, navy, catawba, brown or black, coat front and back elaborately trimmed with fancy black silk braid, piping and buttons of black satin, and braid ornaments, "Directoire" collar finished with satin necklet, coat lined with soft silk and interlined, new model skirt formed of narrow gores, trimmed with braid and buttons to match coat..39.50

No. 80. Three-Piece Tailored Suit, of fine broadcloth, in taupe, catawba, stone, wistaria, navy, brown or black, collar and cuffs of self toned ottoman silk trimmed with buttons of the cloth and silk ornaments, princess dress trimmed to match, gored skirt with felled seams and tailored strappings of the cloth, finished with ornaments..39.50

116   117   118

WOMEN'S FUR COATS.

Sizes 32 to 46.

No. 116. Women's Coat, of black caracul fur, 45 inches long, lined with fine quality brocaded satin, shawl collar and cuffs of same fur and fancy buttons..........................79.50
Same Model, 50 inches...........................89.50
Same Model, 36 inches...........................69.50
Same Model, in black Russian pony skin, 36 inches long....39.50
45 inches long 45.00
50 inches long 59.50

No. 117. Black Caracul Fur Coat, 36 inches long, lined with brocaded satin, collar and cuffs of same fur, trimmed with crochet or fancy buttons 69.50

No. 118. Women's Coat, of black pony skin fur, 36 inches, lined with heavy satin, collar and cuffs of same fur, trimmed with fancy buttons 39.50

Fur, workmanship and linings of superior quality, wear guaranteed.

132 133 134 135

WOMEN'S DRESSY COATS.

Sizes 32 to 44.

No. 132. Stylish Coat, of imported black caracul cloth, semi-fitted, rolling collar and cuffs of same material, finished with fancy braid buttons, lined throughout with satin....................**19.75**

No. 133. Smart Tight Fitting Coat, of broadcloth, in stone, tan, brown, navy, mulberry, catawba, green or black, collar and cuffs of striped velvet to match, edged with braid, embroidered in harmonizing colors, sleeves tucked, coat finished with fancy buttons of the cloth, lined throughout with handsome striped or plain satin.**29.50**

No. 134. Stylish Semi-Fitted Coat, of imported black caracul cloth, directoire collar finished with satin tie, deep cuffs of self material, coat trimmed with handsome cut jet buttons, lined throughout with satin **29.50**

No. 135. Handsome Black Broadcloth Coat, copy of imported model, front, back and sleeves elaborately trimmed with bands of satin braided with soutache, neck edged with velvet, trimming in back forming empire effect, black satin buttons and ornaments.**19.75**

Misses' sizes, 14, 16 and 18 years, same price.

154   155   156   157

MISSES' AND GIRLS' FUR COATS.

No. 154. Black Caracul Fur Coat, selected skins, full length, lined with best quality of brocaded silk, handsome buttons.

Years......	6	8	10	12	14	16
Prices......	74.50	79.50	89.50	98.50	125.00	135.90

No. 154 in French seal fur.

Years......	6	8	10	12	14	16
Prices......	59.50	64.50	69.50	74.50	79.50	89.50

No. 155. French Seal Fur Coat, 45 inches long, fine satin lining . . 59.50

Same Model in black pony skin, sizes 14 to 20 years 45.00

Same Model, black caracul fur, lined with brocaded silk 79.50

No. 157. French Seal Fur Coat, full length, trimmed with handsome buttons and lined with best quality of brocaded silk.

Years......	6	8	10	12	14	16
Prices......	49.50	54.50	59.50	64.50	69.50	79.50

No. 156. Black Pony Skin Coat, 50 inches long, satin lining . 59.50

Same Model, 45 inches long, sizes 14 to 20 years 45.00

Same Model, 36 inches long 39.50

Fur, workmanship and lining of superior quality, wear guaranteed.

Fifth Avenue, New York.

MISSES' AND GIRLS' COATS.

No. 163. Tailored Coat, of diagonal cheviot coating, in navy, gray, brown, green, wine, large patch pockets, velvet collar and cuffs, flannel lined, sizes 6 to 16 years.........................**9.75**

No. 164. Stylish Tailored Coat, of imported all wool coating, in self toned stripes, gray, brown and blue colorings, also plain navy, brown or black vicuna cloth, velvet collar, lined with all wool checked serge, sizes 6 to 14 years..................................**15.75**
16 and 18 years.......................................**18.75**

No. 165. Full Length Tailored Coat, of all wool navy blue chinchilla, velvet collar, lined with gray flannel, sizes 4 to 12 years.......**9.75**

No. 166. Tailored Coat, of all wool coating, self toned herringbone effect, plaid back, in gray or brown colorings, also in plain navy or brown coating, velvet collar, patch pocket, lined in sleeves and yoke with French Venetian, sizes 10 to 14 years...........**15.75**
16 and 18 years......................................**18.75**

No. 167. Dressy Tailored Coat, imported all wool coating, in taupe, smoke, gray, navy, brown or black, velvet collar, patch pockets, strappings of cloth, and coat trimmed front and back with buttons of material and velvet loops, sizes 8 to 16 years............**14.50**

No. 168. Tailored Coat, seven-eighths length, of all wool imported navy blue, gray or red chinchilla, velvet collar, lined with flannel, sizes 4 to 16 years...........................**Special 12.50**

178   179   180   181

MISSES' AND GIRLS' TAILORED SUITS.

No. 178. Three-Piece Tailored Suit, self striped or plain cheviot, in smoke, blue, green, brown or black, semi-fitted coat satin lined and wool interlined, collar and cuffs trimmed with soutache braid, princess dress trimmed with fold, satin strappings, buttons of material, satin tie finished with braid, plaited skirt stitched with tailored strap of material and buttons, sizes 14 to 18 years **19.75**

No. 179. Three-Piece Tailored Suit, of self striped, all wool, two toned or plain serge, in navy, brown, green and wine, coat satin lined and wool interlined, collar and pipings of satin, princess dress trimmed to match, full plaited skirt, sizes 10 to 16 years ...**16.75**

No. 180. Three-Piece Tailored Suit, of French broadcloth, in raspberry, catawba, wistaria, taupe, smoke, green, navy blue, brown, garnet or black, semi-fitted coat, satin lined and wool interlined, collar and cuffs of velvet to match, princess dress trimmed with rows of buttons of the cloth and silk braid loops, piped with satin, sizes 12 to 18 years......................................**34.50**

No. 181. Three-Piece Tailored Suit, of French broadcloth, in taupe, smoke, raspberry, wistaria, catawba, Edison or navy blue, green, brown or black, semi-fitted coat satin lined and wool interlined, trimmed with buttons and satin cord, princess dress scalloped and elaborated with satin cord and buttons to match coat, plaited skirt, strappings of cloth, sizes 14, 16, 18 years........................**39.50**

MISSES' AND GIRLS' FURS.

No. 519. Girl's Imitation Ermine Set, stole scarf and flat pillow muff, sizes 2 to 8 years......................**2.95**

No. 521. Girl's White Thibet Set, stole scarf and flat muff,
Sizes 2 to 8 years, **5.00**

No. 523. Girls' Sable or Natural Gray Squirrel Set, throw scarf and flat pillow muff, sizes 8 to 14 years......................**12.50**

No. 525. Misses' Sable or Natural Gray Squirrel Set, stole collar and rug muff, sizes 12 to 18 years......................**18.50**

No. 527. Misses' Blue, Sable or Black Wolf Set, 48-inch scarf and large flat pillow muff. sizes 12 to 18 years......................**14.50**

No. 529. Misses' White Iceland Fox Set, large rug muff (whole skin), stole to match, sizes 12 to 18 years......................**15.75**

Stole or Muff sold separately if desired.

YOUNG WOMEN'S, MISSES' AND GIRLS' HATS.

No. 101. Nobby Hat, of French felt, trimmed with large ostrich pompom, ribbon loops and band, in black, brown, navy, red or leather color 3.45

No. 103. Mushroom Hat, of velvet, trimmed with full bow of taffeta silk, shirred facing of chiffon, in black, navy, brown, green, red, pink, violet, light blue or white 5.75

No. 105. Mushroom Hat, of fine French felt, trimmed with full ruche and large bow of messaline silk ribbon, in black, brown, navy, green, red or smoke 5.95

No. 107. Mushroom Sailor of fine French felt, in black, brown, navy, leather or red, trimmed with silk velvet band to match .. 1.95

No. 109. Jaunty Hat, of fine French felt, rolling brim, trimmed with two handsome wings and folds of soft silk, colors, black, brown, navy, red, green or smoke 9.75

No. 111. Stylish Hat, of silk beaver felt, trimmed with two large wings and satin ribbon bow, colors, black, brown, green, navy or red 7.95

No. 113. Hat of French Felt, in black, brown, red or navy, brim rolled in front, trimmed with handsome silk polka dot scarf 2.45

No. 115. Smart Hat, of fine French felt, large rolled brim, trimmed with four quills and owl's head, colors, black, brown, navy, red, green or smoke 6.95

No. 140. Mushroom Hat, of French felt, black, brown, navy, green, garnet, cardinal or smoke, medium size brim, trimmed with silk scarf to match 3.75

No. 142. Mushroom Hat, of French felt, large brim, bell-shaped crown, band and binding of stitched satin to match, colors, smoke, brown, red, navy or black 3.95

No. 144. Charlotte Corday Hat, of velvet, taffeta plaited facing edged with plaited ruffle of same, trimmed with large taffeta rosettes in brown, navy, green, violet, red, light blue, pink, white or black 4.50

Felt Hats can be furnished in pearl gray, white or champagne, at an advance of $1.00.

The Art

OF

MILLINERY

A complete series of

PRACTICAL LESSONS

FOR THE

ARTISTE AND THE AMATEUR

By

MME. ANNA BEN YÛSUF

THE MILLINERY TRADE PUBLISHING CO.

13 Astor Place, New York

PREFACE

THERE is no department of women's work more fascinating or more remunerative than millinery, provided she who essays to be a milliner has the talent to manipulate materials and an artistic eye for the harmonious blending of colors; and yet with all these, if there is lacking constructive ability, the road to success is impeded and the ambition to become a creator of fashion in women's headwear is thwarted to no limited extent. To assist those, therefore, who possess talent and desire to perfect themselves in the practical work of millinery, as well as to extend the artistic talent of the trimmer and designer, is the aim of the author of this book. No better pen could attempt such a task with good promise of success than that of Madame Anna Ben-Yûsuf, whose experience as an artistic designer in Paris and London, and whose ability as a preceptress placed her in charge of public and philanthropic institutions in London, where millinery is taught as a science and where she obtained prizes for her work, besides testimonials signed by Members of Parliament and heads of great schools of learning. Madame Ben-Yûsuf was also for several years a preceptress at Pratt Institute, Brooklyn, teaching the art of millinery in all its branches with such success that many of her pupils are now occupying positions of prominence in the trade, either as workers, heads of establishments of their own, or making use in the home circle of the talents developed through this teacher's instrumentality.

Madame Ben-Yûsuf has been a contributor to the columns of The Millinery Trade Review for a number of years as the author of "Hints to Milliners" and "The Milliner in the Workroom," articles which have been greatly appreciated by the readers of this well known journal.

The novice, the artiste, the milliner, the designer and the trimmer will obtain from the pages of this book those helps which will add to their store of knowledge and will greatly benefit them, whether it be in the millinery parlor, trimming room or the home.

CHARLES W. FARMER,
Editor The Millinery Trade Review.

New York, May, 1909.

INTRODUCTION

A LTHOUGH it is best when possible to have personal instruction from a competent teacher, there are many who have neither the time nor opportunity thus to gain the knowledge necessary to success in millinery; it is for such as these therefore that these lessons are compiled.

Millinery is very wide in its scope; this series of lessons might easily be doubled and still leave something to be said; it has therefore been the writer's aim, from the fund of many years' experience, to confine herself to the chief essentials of this fascinating art, which, when thoroughly mastered, will enable the student to work out successfully any new ideas or problems she may encounter. Each season brings new modes, and with these, new methods of handling the materials; though indeed neither may be "new," but merely a revival of some old, old fashion, both in style and workmanship, cleverly adapted to the modes of the day. The technicalities once mastered, the unusual will present no difficulties, and novel ideas will be easily absorbed.

Millinery consists of two branches, the design and the composition. The design is the ART of the work; the composition is the technical putting together of the design, most of which can be done by the "maker;" but it takes an artist to evolve the design. The designer must understand the work of the whole or she cannot direct the maker, and both must have an intimate knowledge of materials and their possibilities, and of these not the least important are what the uninitiated would call "trifles." It is often just one of these "trifles" that give the final touch of true art to the design.

Remember that the mere going through these lessons will not give the requisite proficiency. The examples must be done many times to ensure deftness, lightness of touch, and the speed necessary for acceptability in any workroom. Only the self-confidence that comes with much practice will assure the pupil of her ability to copy Parisian models. This is not only the test, but a most desirable completion to her education as a milliner; an education that will develop her own ability to design, to originate. It may be slow work, but the goal with its fine emoluments is worth all the time and labor we can give it.

The young woman who desires to make her own hats, and those of her family, will find in these,—when the lessons have been mastered,—enough practice to lay the foundation of an accomplishment that, should it ever become necessary, will prove a pleasant and profitable means of livelihood, and in the meantime enable her to evolve accurate copies of Parisian creations at a small part of the importers' prices; though such prices, all expenses taken into consideration, are perfectly fair. Thus, then, to The Artist and The Amateur this book is dedicated by   THE AUTHOR.

THE ART OF MILLINERY

A Series of Practical Millinery Lessons Written Originally
for The Millinery Trade Review by

MME. ANNA BEN-YÛSUF

Late Millinery Instructor at Pratt Institute, Brooklyn, N. Y.

LESSON I

DRAFTING BUCKRAM FRAMES

FRAMES are now to be had ready for use, of the finest quality and in all the most exclusive shapes, as well as those suitable for medium and cheap trade, both in infinite variety; and if an importer or designer has a special novelty, the manufacturers will make and reserve this pattern for the designer; there is therefore far less frame-making done in workrooms than there was a couple of decades ago; but designers and copyists frequently find it necessary to alter shapes; and also in copying a model the frame has usually to be made. An extra frame is sent with every model that comes over, and if the buyers insist on getting the model frame with every pattern hat they purchase, the milliner can easily copy it; otherwise the measurements must be carefully taken, without in the least disarranging the hat.

The designer in a frame factory drafts his patterns by geometric rules; he has usually plenty of table room. The milliner has only limited space, and therefore finds a simpler method more expedient; but we will consider both methods, that the pupil may use either or both, as may seem expedient.

To Draft a Frame on Geometrical Principles

Begin by copying a simple shape; take and note down all measurements, i. e., Size of head line, circumference and diameter. The circumference is, roughly speaking, three times the diameter, but, accurately measured, it will be found to be a seventh more. For instance—

| | Diameter. | |
Circumference.	Back to Front.	Side to Side.
18	6	5½
17	5½	5¼
16	5¼	5

and intermediate measurements in corresponding ratio.

An elliptical or oval crown fits the head better than the round form, but very small head sizes are usually round, and fitted to the head by bandeaux. Some crowns that are round at the tip are fitted to an oval head line.

If the side band of crown is quite straight, the tip (top), being the same size as the head, no separate pattern is needed; the piece that comes out of brim at head line serves as pattern for top of crown, and the side of crown is a straight strip cut to length of circumference with one-half inch laps added, and of the required depth.

If, however, the upper circle of crown differs in size from the headline circumference, this circumference and diameter must be noted down.

For the brim take entire diameter from back to front, and side to side, also at an even distance between these points take diagonal measures across; noting all down accurately.

Next take diameter of head size *on under side of hat*, back to front and side to side; then the brim from the edge in to the head line, front, back, right side, left side, and between if necessary—as some special curve of brim depends often on these measures, as for instance in the "Gainsboro," boat shapes, etc. (See Figs. 3 and 6.)

8

"Laying Out" the Shape

Take a sheet of pattern paper more than twice as large as the largest diameter of brim; fix it on a table or large drawing board with drawing pins; in the upper half rule a perfect square, each side measuring the largest diameter of your hat brim. (See Fig. 1.) Now rule diagonal lines from corner to corner, and one perpendicular and one horizontal line from middle to middle of each line of the square, so all the lines cross at the exact middle of square; mark this dot 1 (see Fig. 2); and mark the straight lines A and B. Let us suppose your brim is 6 inches front depth, 3 inches back, with a 6 inch diameter of headsize from front to back, and 5½ from side to side; that gives you a largest diameter of entire brim of 15 inches; therefore

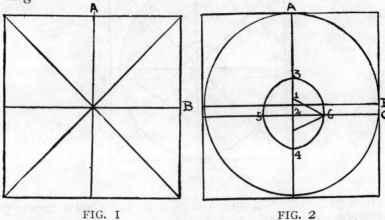

FIG. 1   FIG. 2

your square must measure 15 inches along each side. Within this square draw a circle touching each side, draw by pinning a string in exact middle and holding pencil on string at required length. Now measure from top of line A where it touches the square, 6 inches down and put dot 3; measure 3 inches up from base of line A and put dot 4. Find exact middle from 3 to 4 and make dot 2 for center of headsize. Take measure from dots 1 to 2, and take same from line B

9

downward on each side of square dot and rule across for line C. (See Fig. 2.)

Now from dot 2 measure to each side along line C the half of cross headsize which in the example is 2¾ inches and place dots 5 and 6.

To draw an elliptical headline measure from dots 2 to 4, get same measure obliquely by letting the ruler touch dot 6 and the other end of measure strike line A; rule from 6 upward in same way, mark these dots X; set the compass on these dots and drawing to right and left, a true oval can be obtained, taking the longest point for radius, and touching each dot of the diameter.

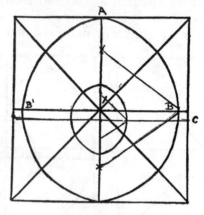

FIG. 3

A second circle for tip is done in the same way, moving the compass a little up or down in proportion, and an oval brim is also obtained by this rule, taking a central two-fourths of longest diameter as pivots, from which to swing compass. (See Fig. 3.)

If compasses are not at hand tie a knot in the end of a bit of string, push a drawing pin through knot, and stick firmly on the dot instead of compass point, measure string to the point of radius, twist it round a bit of pencil meeting this point and draw circle or oval as required.

10

It is safest to swing curves from each straight line towards the diagonals ensuring their meeting accurately there; measured dots will ensure both sides being alike, or eccentric, if so required; and the curves swung according. (See Figs. 3 and 4.)

For the brim stick compass or pin at dot 1, and taking the radius from A swing curve towards B, but rest on dot on diagonal; move pencil to B and swing up, meeting on diagonal; swing to B1 in same way then from A1 upward; this gives you outlines of brim and headsize. (See Fig. 4.) Fig. 3 gives the lines and points of radius for a long or boat shaped brim.

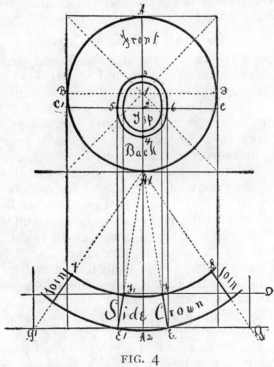

FIG. 4

For a conical crown (a crown the tip of which is smaller than the headsize), draw a circle *within* the headline, the middle space representing the top of crown.

11

When the crown tip is small, of course there is a wider space between the two circles, than if the difference is slight, and if the crown tip is larger, as in a "Bell" or "Tam" crown; the second circle is drawn *outside* the headline. (See Figs. 4 and 5.)

When the space between the two circles is less than one-half inch, the straight lines running down will be longer than if the space exceeds that measurement. The reason is that when the slope between top of crown and headline is great, a shorter radius is required to get the circle and the more nearly alike the two measurements are, the larger will be the circumference of circle from which the section is taken, and the further from brim must be the lowest curve.

To Draft a Conical Crown

To get a conical crown draw a second circle within the headline. Rule off a second square below and adjoining the upper one and of the same dimensions; find middle of lowest line, and extend line $A1$ a little below this point, calling it $A2$. Measure upward from lowest line of square on $A2$ the depth of crown, say 3 inches, and dot, measure the same from lowest line of square up on side lines, dot and rule across, call this line D. Measure from edge of brim C and $C1$ to dots 6 and 5, and mark off the same measures from side lines along lowest line of square towards center and dot; call these points E and $E1$. Measure along line C to inner circle, and dot off same measure *along line D* from side lines of lower square; now from dots 5 and 6 rule lines down to dots E and $E1$ on lowest line of second square, and from inner circle on line C rule down to dots on line D, rule oblique lines from dot $A1$ to E and F which will give you slope of crown. (See Fig. 4.)

Rule off a small square (depth of crown) outside the large square, using lowest and side lines of square, and line D, and add another perpendicular line. From dot $A1$ rule a diagonal line which will cut through the lower outside corners of these squares; this line gives you the

slope of crown at join; call these lines G and G1. Now
set compass or pin at A1, take radius from E or E1,
and swing curve so it touches both these points, comes
a little below lowest line of square at A2, and runs
through G and G1. (See Fig. 4.) From this point
measure up on the diagonal line the depth of crown
and mark 7 and 8; keep the pin at A1 and swing the
upper curve by taking radius to F and curving a little
below line D in the middle on line A2, ending on each
side at dots 7 and 8.

When a wider radius is indicated, lines G and G1
must be swung out further, and the line taken from a
different point, dots 1 or 2 or even higher. The re-
spective measures of head and tip lines will indicate the
difference to be allowed in the two lines of side of crown.

To Draft a Shallow Wide Top Crown

In Fig. 5 we use the same brim with a wide top
"Bell" crown, 2 inches high; therefore, we make the
second circle *outside* the headline, then proceed the same
as in Fig. 4; but as it is for a lower, wider crown, we
must find a wider radius, which means a longer distance
from the point where we set the pin to the pencil, which
must touch the given point of radius.

Of course, any one who has studied geometry will
know how to find the corresponding arc to any given
circle; but no one expects milliners to take degrees in
geometry, so we will say the quickest way to find the
side slope of crown is to stick the pin on line A2 and
measure to either side half the circumference of larger
crown line and dot; then on line D from A2 measure
to either side the smaller crown line; if these dots come
beyond the small square on either side, add another small
square of the same size, and lay the ruler so it exactly
cuts through the two dots; where these diagonal lines
meet in the upper square will be the point to place your
pin to get the radius, and this will be from the same
points in lower square as first example. (See Fig. 5.)

13

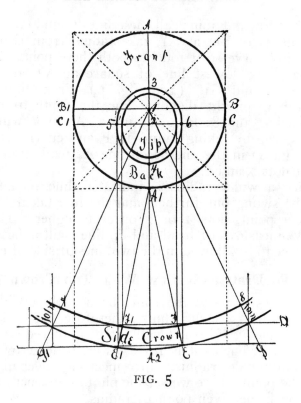

FIG. 5

Plain Sailor Crown

Of course, a perfectly round crown is easy to do, as the pin is set in the exact middle, the radius taken from the required edge of circle, and the pencil or compass swung round.

Every curve is the section of a circle, large or small. Take a cart-wheel for instance; divide the rim into six equal parts; you will require a radius represented by the measure from axle to edge to get this *section* correctly, just as much as if you had to draw the entire wheel.

Instruments both for curves and rectangles can be bought, which simplify this work considerably.

Bandeaux that are to be shaped like the sides of crowns are drafted, and cut in the same way.

14

In Fig. 6 the various points to place compass and get radius for an eccentric brim are shown, the brim narrow on one side and deep with upward curve on the other.

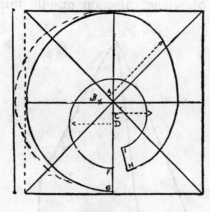

FIG. 6

Simpler Method of Drafting Frames

Pattern paper, pencil, measuring tape, ruler, and scissors are all that you need for this.

To get the square, which is to be of the largest diameter of hat as before directed, mark off on the paper and cut out. Fold over evenly each way to make a square one-quarter the size of open square (See Fig. 7); fold over into a three-cornered wedge, so that the cut edges come together; fold over again, so the paper is a long, narrow, arrow-shaped wedge, with fine point. (See Fig. 8). Measure from the point C, up the shortest side to B, and, measuring up the longer side to A, dot to same measure as short side; measure also the same up exact middle (a ruled line ensures accuracy), and cut off top of wedge in a curve from B to A through central dot. This gives you a perfect round of any size required, and the creased lines are ready for variations if desired. (See Figs. 8-9.)

Do not unfold the paper, however, but cut out the headline, thus: If the headsize is to be 17 inches, the diameter of a round headsize will be 5½ inches, therefore measure *half* this: i. e., 2¾ inches from point C up on each side of wedge, also on middle line, and make

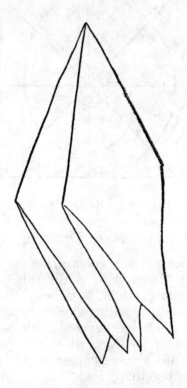

FIG. 7

dots D, E, F; cut off the tip in a curve through these dots; this gives you the headsize, and top of crown, if this is to be the same size as headline; and a straight strip will be required for side of crown. (See Fig. 9.)

If you want a brim wider in front than at back, open the paper after having cut the edge circle; measure at

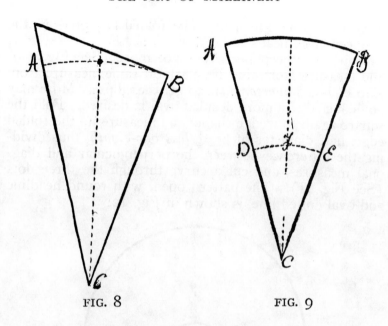

FIG. 8   FIG. 9

middle line from edge down for width of front brim,
and from opposite edge for width of back brim (taking
care, however, to leave a good proportion for the headsize); fold over so these two marks come *exactly over*

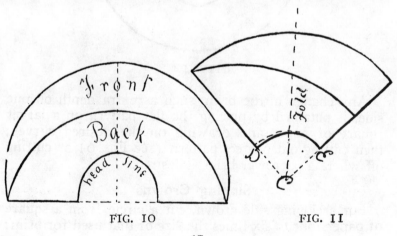

FIG. 10   FIG. 11

17

each other (See Fig. 10). The folded line gives us the new center of headsize.

Now fold the paper over once more (See Fig. 11), and measure from C to E; mark off same measure from C to D, *less a quarter inch,* to get the ellipse. More may be deducted if a more decided oval is desired. Fold the square again to wedge shape, and measure up the folded edge, half diameter of head, *less one-eighth,* thus dividing the difference between the perpendicular and diagonal measures, and cut a curve through the three dots (See Fig. 11). The pattern open, with round headline and oval dotted line, is shown in Fig. 12.

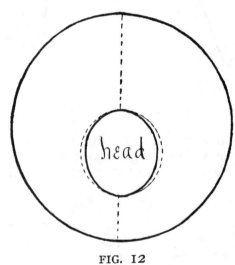

FIG. 12

Any change in the brim, such as extra depth on one side, is obtained by placing the flat pattern on a larger square of paper and drawing on the desired curves; then cutting out perfect pattern (see Fig. 6) or cutting off where a narrower brim is desired.

Sloping Crowns

For a sloping side crown, cut a circle from a square of paper four to six times the size of that used for brim;

the deeper the slope the smaller the square needed.
Fold and cut round as for brim; then measure required
depth of crown from the *edge in,* at each side and the

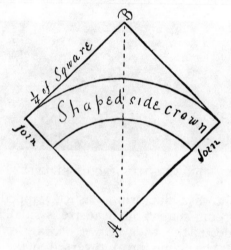

FIG. 13

middle; mark and cut out (Fig. 13). From this circle
measure off your exact *head* circumference, half to each
side of the diagonal line running from A to B: The
diagram shows a quarter section of entire square, which
will be found more practical than the entire square, and
from this the half pattern can be cut; along the inner
circle measure off and dot measure of tip, if conical; if
"Bell," reverse the measurements, and cut off section
in line with square.

It will be easily seen that such sections can be cut as
wide or narrow as desired, and a few experiments will
show the pupil the right relation of crowns to brims and
headsizes.

Eccentric Frames

The eccentric curves, ripples, and contractions of
shapes are obtained by either gores let in or taken out,
or slashes, which are lapped and sewn over more or less
to get the shape desired; for a deeply turned up "poke"

the headsize is cut 2 inches larger than required, and a wedge 1½ inches across widest part at *headline* is taken out of the front, the two edges lapped and stitched.

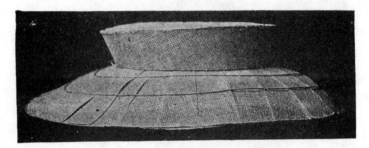

FIG. 14—MUSHROOM SHAPE

Fig. 14 shows a flat brim, slashed, lapped and sewn into a mushroom shape; the headsize is small, fitted with a deep bandeau; the wide crown has a *slightly* shaped side band. The same brim reversed makes a saucer-brim sailor. The crown may be "Bell" or plain. The

FIG. 15
FLAT PATTERN OF MUSHROOM SHAPE

brim is 15 inches diameter, the widest part, 5½ inches, coming on the left, raised here by a 3-inch bandeau; the narrowest part of brim comes at the right back—4 inches—where the bandeau decreases to 1½ inches. The wide crown, with slightly sloping side, is set on beyond the headline. The slashes in the brim are lapped only just enough to hold the stitches, at back and left a trifle more to give a more decided curve.

The edge wire, and two additional circular wires, hold the slits firm.

Fig. 15 shows the **flat pattern** slashed for shaping.

Fig. 16 is a brim cut from same size square, but differently shaped. The deepest part of brim—5½ inches—comes at the left back, the narrowest part—3½ inches—on the right near the front, leaving a head-size of 5 inches diameter, less ½ an inch from side to side. The crown is 3 inches high, the tip larger than

FIG. 16

the head, slightly shaped side band, which is cut a straight strip in two parts and lapped to shape back and front. Fig. 17 shows the flat pattern.

21

To Make Buckram Frames

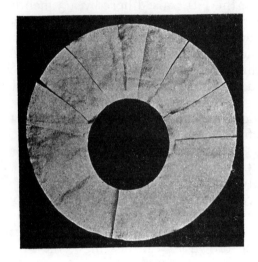

FIG. 17

FLAT PATTERN OF TURNED-UP SHAPE

Never allow turnings on patterns; lay smoothly on buckram, sparterie or cape net, pin firmly and cut out. No edge turnings are allowed, but three-quarters of an inch is allowed at the head; this is snipped at one-inch intervals to the head line; and a half inch is allowed at each end of the side crown for lapping. The

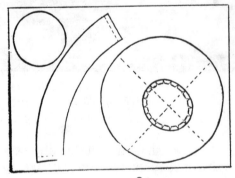

FIG. 18

snipped margin, at head line is turned up inside the crown.

In cutting cape net, a firmer edge is obtained by allowing just enough margin to turn over all edge wires, and backstitching (long) these in, instead of button-hole-sewing them on as in buckram frames.

Wire around edge of brim with strong wire, set on

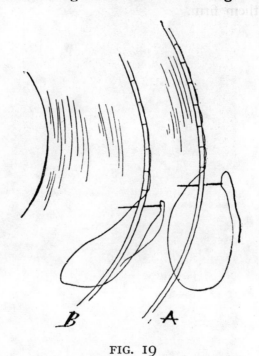

FIG. 19

the *edge* with "blanket" stitch, stitches one-eighth of an inch long, the tie coming *on the wire;* wire around the headline flat, with one-quarter inch long loop stitches (Fig. 19). Lap and sew side crown, and wire round both edges same as brim; set on and sew in place with half-inch long button-hole stitches, unless the crown comes much over the brim; then attach at six or eight places only. Last sew tip on side crown, with one-

23

eighth inch button-hole stitches, taking care, if oval, to get this exactly to back and front.

In cape net frames a quarter inch should be allowed around the tip; this to be turned down and sewn flat under top wire of side crown; it will fit better if the margin is snipped.

Wide brims will need extra wires, rings and braces to keep them firm.

LESSON II

MAKING WIRE FRAMES

WIRE frames are made entirely by measurements, and, the method and use of tools once mastered, are really easier to make than buckram frames. If, however, the milliner designs a new shape, it is best to do so in paper, or buckram; then from this make the wire frame. If the frame is made experimentally, the edge wire should be lightly tied, the cross wires not clipped permanently tight, nor the other rings tied on finished with the tie wire, so that all may be adjusted, then when lines and form are right all fastenings are secured immovably.

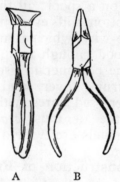

A   B
FIG. I
CUTTERS "A"
PLIERS "B"

The Tools

The tools necessary for making wire frames are a pair of small wire cutters, and a small pair of pliers, costing respectively 40 cents and 15 cents. There is a tool that combines the two, but it is not practical for millinery, as the points are necessarily wider and thicker, and do not lay hold of the fine wires, nor

25

bend intricate angles as neatly as the finer points of the true pliers. (Fig. 1, Cutters, A; Pliers, B.)

A narrow tape-measure, having inches and ⅛ths on one side and 1/16 of the inch on the other; avoid those that unroll from a case, the simple tailors' tape is best. Of wire, one needs for a nice frame four different kinds. A ring of thickly covered edge wire; this is a strong wire covered first with layers of cotton thread, running along the wire, over which is spun a covering of silk floss. (The same kind of wire, but softer, is used to edge hats, and run into "cordings.") The round rings of the frame should be of a heavier number of wire than the brace wires, the eight wires that form the spokes of the wheel, all crossing in the center of top of crown, as these have to be several times bent. Then there is the "tie" wire, which comes like coarse thread on a spool; all these are silk covered. But there are cotton and even paper covered wires, and uncovered tie wire, which is used for the cheapest frames, and is good enough for practice.

It is well for the beginner to use the tools on bits of wire, cutting, turning over, and clipping the turns tight, also tying crossed wires with the tie wire cut in 1-inch lengths; the tie must *cross* the wires twice; then the two little ends are twisted together and turned under.

Construction of Frames

The number of round wires in a frame varies according to the size and shape; there is always the edge and head wire; then if crown and brim are in one, there is the crown wire; if the crown is deep, there is a second wire between head and crown; if the brim is wide there may be two more round wires between edge and head; in a medium size, one is enough, and in a narrow brim none extra is needed. Often one side of a frame is much deeper than the rest of the brim; in that case one or even two part wires are put in. (Fig. 2.) This is also often necessary in toque and bonnet

26

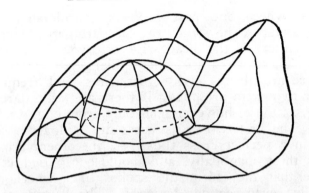

FIG. 2—FRAME SHOWING SEPARATE BRIM
AND CROWN. EXTRA BRACE IN FLUTE
AND EXTRA PART RING WIRE

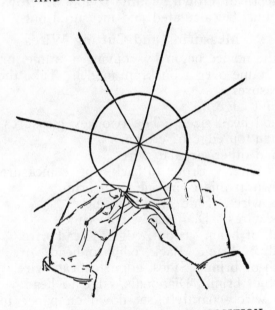

FIG. 3. CROSS WIRES TIED IN POSITION.
TOP OF CROWN RING "TIED" ON,
SHOWING ACTION OF TURNING
WIRE WITH PLIERS FOR SIDE
OF CROWN

frames, where one part projects considerably more than the rest of the structure; the part wires being secured either to the head wire or two of the brace wires. These wires are called "fillers."

There are always eight cross wires, and frequently one or two extra are put in if there are wide flares, as in Fig. 2; these, however, run only from edge to head wire. The first two cross wires are laid across each other in a perfect cross thus: +; the others are laid across these diagonally, and should be so tied in the middle that they form the spokes of a wheel, with (usually) even sections between. The lengths of the spokes, however, on each side of the center, depend on the measurements of brim, back, front, right side, left side, depth of crown, width of top of crown, all of which must be calculated and measured out. (Fig. 3.)

Measuring and Cutting Wires

Let the novice begin by copying a frame, or making a wire frame over a buckram model. Take the following measures:

Around edge.

Around head size. (The two key measures.)

Around top edge of crown.

Around other circular wires.

Cross wires. Front to back, entire measure including crown, if this is in one with brim.

Cross wires. Side to side, same.

Cross wires. Diagonal wires, same.

Width of brim. Front, edge to head wire.

Width of brim. Back, edge to head wire.

Width of brim. Sides, edge to head wire.

Width of brim. Diagonals, edge to head wire.

Each wire separately, set down on paper for reference. Add measures of:

Depth of crown; if this is deeper at any one place carefully note it down, together with the cross wire *where the extra height* is required.

Measure across top of crown. If this is a perfect

round the diameter will be the same back to front, and side to side, but if it is an oval, or other form, each measure must be taken the same as for the brim.

One and one-half inches extra is allowed in cutting the cross wires, this is a ½-inch for turn over at each end, and ½-inch for "take up" in the turns or bends.

Now cut your edge wire, allowing two inches for lapping in a satin wire, and three in a hard wire. In cutting, take care to *cut clean*, as bending hooks in the end of the wires and ravelling the covering makes untidy frames. The satin wire may be lapped and sewn, but hard wire must have the *ends* of the lap neatly twisted over with a bit of tie wire; it is unnecessary to twist the lap all along. Thus make all the rings you need for your frame, lay them down inside each other, so you can see at a glance which to take up. In the crown rings a lap of 1½ inches is sufficient, and all laps should come at the back of the frame.

Now cut the cross wires, allowing 1½ inches extra on each, lay them down in the position on each other as you cut them, so that no mistake is possible.

To Make the Frame

It is best to tie the front to back and side wires first, then secure the diagonals in place separately, being careful to allow on each one the necessary measure

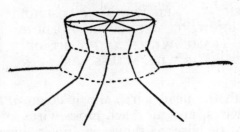

FIG. 4.   CROSS WIRES BENT OUT FOR
BRIM.   DOUBLE BELL CROWN

from the center out.   (Fig. 3.)   Now measure from center out the *half* diameter of top of crown, if a round all will be the same, but if an oval (Fig. 6) or boat-shape crown, the measures will be longer from back to front than from side to side. Bend each wire downward at the indicated measure, with the *pliers,* holding as shown in Fig. 3.

The next step is to bend the wires out at the head-line; for this measure downward on each wire from the first bend the depth of crown required. If this is a simple crown like Fig. 5, all the measures will be the same, but if the crown is higher at any place, this measure must be carefully given at the proper brace, and each wire bent out in the opposite direction to the first bend. (See Fig. 4.) We are now ready to lay in our round wires.

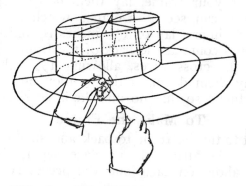

FIG. 5. ALL WIRES IN POSITION,
SHOWING METHOD OF HOLDING
FRAME WHILE TYING BIT OF
TIE WIRE ACROSS WIRES

Begin with the head wire; slip it down *outside* onto the cross wires, and tie each cross wire to the ring with a bit of tie wire, as shown in Fig. 5, having a care that the spaces between are equal. If the top of crown —as in a bell shape—is larger than the head line, the ring can be left open and joined after being laid in position on the skeleton. In Fig. 4 a bell shape is shown, which has *two* bends in side of crown; when this is used a ring must be placed at each bend.

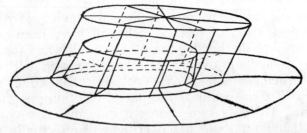

FIG. 6.   SHOWING (SEPARATE) OVAL CROWN

When the crown is oval, however, the spaces from front and back to side wires will be a little wider than the two side spaces, the same proportions being retained in the brim. (See Fig. 6.)   If this is much flared the extra brace mentioned before will be needed.

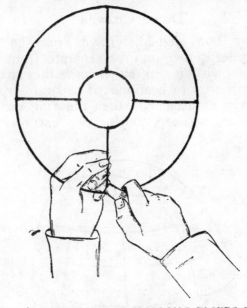

FIG. 7.   METHOD OF HOLDING PLIERS FOR CLIPPING BRACE OVER EDGE WIRES

31

Now we put in our edge wire, and this is the test if the cross wires have been correctly measured. The 1½ inches allowed on the length of each cross wire, have, of course, been equally divided, leaving ¾ of an inch to each side; of this ¼ inch will have been taken up in forming the bends; the other ½ inch at each end is now *turned up* over the edge wire, and with the pliers turned flat on *itself*, enclosing the edge wire firmly with a close clip of the pliers. Nothing is gained by having a double twist here; it only makes a clumsy bunch, that no amount of covering will effectually conceal; the wire must be neatly and evenly turned, and firmly pinched down; if the end turns down below the wire, cut it off quite close. (See Fig. 7.) Secure all eight wires in place, then add extra brace wires, or part circular wires if needed; and the middle wire around crown. (Figs. 2 and 5.)

Dome Crowns

Dome, or bowl-shaped, crowns may be shallow, medium, or deep; they may be separate from brim, or made in one with it; in either case they are *curved* evenly from center to headline; if separate from brim, the head wire is attached; then the ring near center, and if medium or deep, one or two extra rings mid-

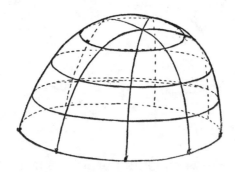

FIG. 8. DOME CROWN

32

way between these two, are put on, as in Fig. 8. These must be measured so that they hold the bowl in the required form, which may be wide, or more conical in shape.

If the crown and brim are in one the measures must be taken in the same way from center to headline, the wires *curved* and then bent out for brim.

Separate Brims

These are usually made when the crown is to be larger at the base than the head size of brim, or when the brim is of such eccentric form that it would be difficult to cover it with the crown on; in this case a one-inch band is turned up at the head size (see Figs. 2 and 9), which, when covered with crinoline, forms a foundation to which is attached the rest of covering, head lining and bandeau.

The same band, but deeper, is shown in Fig. 6, where the base of the crown forms one supporting

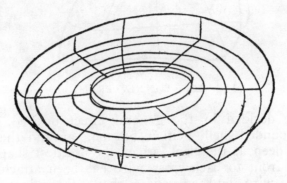

FIG. 9.   TURBAN BRIM FOR LARGE
SEPARATE CROWN

ring of the brim; net shirred on wire cords formed the hat, therefore the simplest skeleton was enough as frame, but a wider inner band, covered with cape net, was necessary.

In **Fig.** 9 we show a wide turban brim with head

33

band; the suitable crown would be wide and a little higher than the "gallery," i. e., that part of a turban brim that turns up around the edge. This shape, with headband reversed, forms also a mushroom shape.

Bonnet Frames

The small bonnet frame is but little used now, except for widows' mourning, and far less than formerly even here, but the method of making is useful to know. The edge wire is the first; this is bent into the desired shape (see Fig. 10); the back may be deep or shallow; if shallow, the cross wire that runs from the middle front to middle back must be cut longer, and curved down. The length of edge wire from middle front to "ears," i. e., the corner where the wire turns upward,

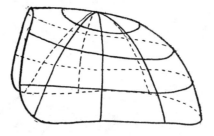

FIG. 10.   BONNET FRAME

must be decided by the general effect desired, but a neatly rounded shell, neither too long around the face nor too deep at the back, gives the prettiest shape.

After front to back cross wire has been attached to the edge wire, and curved to shape, the side to side brace is put in, then the diagonal wires, which run from the ears over to the opposite side, half way between front and side wires, all, of course, crossing and being tied at top of crown. A ring is then set on top of crown; the diameter of this depends on the size of the shape, but about three inches is the usual measure. One other round wire is always needed;

34

sometimes, as in Fig. 10, two are used, because of the *depth* of the frame; these are as shown, attached to the edge wire at back; if only one is needed, and the *back is shallower,* this may be a ring coming half way all round between the crown wire and edge, except, of course, at the ears which are not taken into consideration here.

If a coronet is desired on such a bonnet, extra must be allowed for this on the *cross wires,* and these bent up at the desired angle from the edge, an extra edge wire giving the outline of coronet edge; this is clipped tightly over the bonnet edge at the ears.

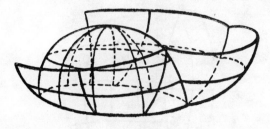

FIG. 10A

Child's Bonnet

For a child's close bonnet the edge wire is bent as shown in Fig. 11. To get the measurements, take these as directed in the lesson on children's millinery, i. e., around the face, over the head from front to back, around the head from side to side, and around the base of head from in front of and below each ear. The edge wire is in one (1), joined at back of neck. Put in first the wire from front to back, (2) next the one from side to side, (3) tie at back where they cross; these will be your keys, for the other wires, which may be cut approximately, tied on at the top, then curved to the right form, and tied at side and neck. In the model there are three each way; they are numbered in the order in which it is best to place them,

35

These forms for children's bonnets are also made of tape wire, called also ribbon and "taste" wire; this is used flat, and *sewed* at the intersections. In either case, all wire ends must be left *outside* of frame, or they are apt to work through and scratch the child. Made only to the size of the second wire around face (4), the corners *rounded*, as in the lady's bonnet, also the back shortened, it gives us the crown of a granny bonnet, to which can be added a flaring brim, either made in one with the crown; or a *corded* brim is set on by the milliner. (The writer has found flat featherbone an excellent substitute for wire for children's bonnets

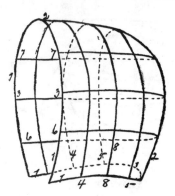

FIG. II
CHILD'S CLOSE BONNET

and hats, as it rebounds into shape when crushed, which wire will not do. For small fur hats and the little fashionable evening toques it is equally practical.)

Let the learner look at a number of well-made frames, and notice how the lines are formed by edge wires and braces, and how the supporting rings or part rings are put in.

Methods of Holding and Handling

The easiest way is always the best way, and the *right* way is always the *quickest* way. If a thing feels awkward in the doing, be sure you are not doing it right. It takes a little practice to use the tools so that they will do their work neatly and swiftly; the cutters must be opened just enough to pass the wire between, which must be severed with one firm clip, pressing the two handles together in the bowl of the right hand. (See Figs. 3 and 7.) The pliers must be used in the same way, but their points are used in place of finger and thumb, and with the firm pressure of the whole 'hand, hold more strength, and a firmer, as well as neater, grip than the fingers.

Keep all wires even, allow no "kinks." A firm, even pressure with the thumb will straighten the ring out, when it can easily be bent quite straight. Unless first bent straight, wires will twist, and if made up thus, the frame will have a squirm that nothing but re-making will remove.

Practice the tying; one twist each way across the wires is sufficient, if the ends are firmly twisted and turned under, and 1 inch is enough.

Frames of Twisted Wire

Many frames are made without tie wire; for these the cross wires are of much softer wire, as these are *twisted once* around the ring wire, where in the other method the tie is used. In this method a half an inch must be allowed extra for every turn, and the wire must be held *very* firmly, at the right length required, together with the ring, and the twist made with the other hand. It is one turn only, and this must be so close that it holds the ring firmly. It requires much practice to do this and not let either wire slip, which would spoil the lines and proportions of the shape.

Proportions

To get the right proportions relatively of round and cross wires, remember the rules given in the making of buckram frames, i. e., that the circumference of any given part is three times—and a seventh—that of the diameter. Thus, if your crown is 7 inches across, the ring wire that encircles it must be 22 inches plus two added for lapping. If your brim is 14 inches across from front to back, *and side to side,* the edge wire will be three and a seventh times this, which is 44 inches; to this is added the two or more inches for lapping. If, however, the crown is oval, allowance must be made for this, and if the brim is flared, several inches should be allowed and the frame shaped in the making.

Machine-Made Frames

In imitation of the above methods a clever machine has been invented, adjustable to any required form, and, when once mastered, proving swifter, and more accurate than the fingers; it is used in many factories, and by manufacturing milliners, and is therefore well worth while learning.

Parisian Frames

Parisian wire shapes often have a covering of tulle shirred over the wires, it is folded lengthwise along the middle over the edge wire, the two layers shirred together below the wire, and fulled a little as the work proceeds; the material is then drawn smoothly down and shirred below the second wire, then the next and cut neatly beyond the head wire, which is covered with the piece shirred over the crown.

In England and America we cover wire frames according to what is going on them, but one of the nicest materials is horsehair (crinoline) gauze, especially under tulle.

LESSON III

COVERING OF FRAMES

SOME shapes are suitable for plain covering; some, by reason of their eccentric lines, it is not possible to cover plain; for such shapes one resorts to folds, shirrings, or draped effects, each of which will be treated of in turn.

The buckram frame, to be plain covered, should be of simple form, so that no join, or at most only one, may be needed to fit the covering to the brim.

If the brim is very wide, or is to be curved up, or down, in any place, it will be necessary to put "braces" where needed. These are just bars of wire set across the brim with a button-hole stitch, either in form of flat-ended pear-shaped loops, or straight bars (see Fig. 1), the ends of which are turned sharp along the edge wire for about an inch and sewn firmly to this, the other end running an inch up against the crown. The

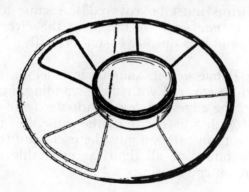

FIG. 1—SHOWING "BRACES" STRAIGHT
AND IN LOOP FORM; ALSO MUSLIN
BINDS AND COVERS ON WIRES

39

loop is carried from an inch up the crown to the edge wire, running parallel with this for about 3 inches, then turning back towards the crown, where the space between the two wires is only 1½ inches.

After the braces are on they must be covered with bias strips of thin interlining crinoline, and in the use of Panne velvet, silk, satin, or broadcloth, thin sheet wadding is to be used over the muslin, or the wires will be outlined through the material; baste the coverings on with very fine thread.

After all braces are covered, the edge wire is bound with bias muslin cut 1¼ inches wide, folded over double, and this double muslin clasped and *stretched* over the edge wire and basted on below it. After this is on, cut another bias muslin strip, 1½ inches wide, and *stretch single* over the first bind; baste this at its *lowest edge;* the first gives roundness to the edge, the second is needed to sew to, as you cannot sew your velvet to the stiff buckram. (See Fig. 1.) The edge of the crown, which in hand-made frames is always wired, must be clasped with a strip of muslin, as shown in cut; if properly stretched, it need only be basted round on top of the crown; the side will cling. Circular wires on brims must be covered the same as braces; by stretching *one edge* of the strip the circular form is obtained, and it is quickly basted on with a long "cat" stitch.

In using Panne velvet, silks or broadcloth, the entire frame must be covered with sheet-wadding, fitted on by the pattern, the edges cut level with the frame, and the edge bound with a bias strip of the same, left raw edge, of course; very fine thread must be used, and the *basting* stitches not pulled at all tight, as even this will show through the outer covering.

Wire Frames

If these are to be used for plain covered hats (though this is not desirable), they must be covered with muslin cut to pattern, *on both sides,* then with wadding, if necessary, as described. Cape net frames need more bracing than buckram or sparterie, but they make the nicest hats. French willow *cloth* is excellent for covering wire frames for plain fitted velvet, etc., being very light, smooth and firm.

Taking the Patterns

If the pupil has studied and learned the making of buckram frames, the taking of patterns will be an easy matter, but for those who have not we will give two or three methods applicable to different shapes.

Many under brims can be stretched on direct from the piece of velvet, without first taking a pattern; pinned round to the crinoline bind, cut round with a ½-inch margin beyond the hat edge; but, unless the crown is taken out, the pattern must be taken for the upper brim piece.

For brims that are curved in at one place and flat at another it is best to measure across for the largest diameter and get a perfect round pattern, as directed for the making of frames; this round is to be pinned on the under brim, and by plaits and slits fitted snug and smooth to the brim, the edge and head lines being cut flush with the frame.

Never allow any turnings in patterns.

It follows that such a pattern cannot be cut flat from the velvet without a join; this must be made to come at the least conspicuous place and where the join is shortest.

Sometimes it is best to stretch the *upper* side of a brim, as in a block mushroom shape; in this case the crown must be taken off, the under facing put in first, cut by a pattern that *fits the edge,* and the material *stretched* till it fits into the curve, in which it is held by tiny invisible stitches in the material, and long ones on the upper surface of the frame. The upper brim piece is then stretched on, the crown covered and put on after.

41

The same method is used in up-turned brims that bulge; the upper is here put on first, and secured in the curves by long stitches on the uncovered side; the tiny ones on the goods, being of matching silk, they really do not show, and there is no other way to compel the material to cling to the frame. Before removing the pattern from the frame, carefully mark F., B., R., L., for front, back, right and left side, and mark the frame to correspond. Note also whether you take the pattern over or under the brim. Do the same with the crown pieces, bringing the join of the side crown where the trimming is to come. Some milliners glue velvet to frames, but it is dangerous and not a desirable method, though the blocked hats are made so.

Cutting Out the Material

In placing the patterns on the material, especially velvet, all must be placed *the same way of the pile,* so that the whole hat will shade one way; there is a difference of taste in this; some like to brush forward, some backward, from the edge; personally, we prefer to brush from the head out, as this is least likely to disarrange the trimmings if a small velvet whisk is used.

If you will look at Fig. 2, you will see that the "front"

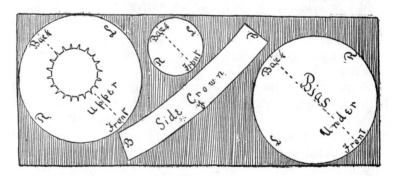

FIG. 2—PATTERN PLACED ON VELVET; BIAS LINE RUNNING
FROM BACK TO FRONT IN EACH PIECE ALIKE

of each piece is on the same direction of the *bias* pile; in this illustration the brim is alike on both sides; therefore the pattern may be safely so placed, but if there is the least difference, it is safest to first cut the upper brim, cutting out at the headline, then by placing this on another piece of the velvet, the same way of the pile, *face to face* or back to back, and cutting the under facing by this, but *not* cutting out the headsize, we ensure the correct pieces for both sides; otherwise it is quite possible to cut two for one side.

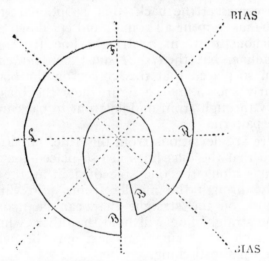

FIG. 3—BRIM DEEPLY CURVED UP ON LEFT
SIDE. BIAS LINES RUN OBLIQUELY
THROUGH, JOIN COMING ON
STRAIGHT LINE AT BACK

Use single-face canton flannel for practice.

In cutting the material from pattern allow a one-half inch margin beyond the edge, and one inch at the headline, this to be snipped in at 1-inch intervals to the pattern headline. (See Fig. 2.) The same is to be allowed when stretching materials over frames, either brims, or tops of crowns.

The reason for leaving the under facing with crown piece in is that the piece may be stretched out *perfectly smooth*, the edges pinned, trimmed down to the ½-inch margin or even less, turned in and slipstitched to the upper part; then the crown piece is cut out with the 1-inch margin, snipped to the head-line, the snips turned up inside the crown and sewn.

In cutting the "tip" allow a half-inch margin; on the side of crown the same, on each side, and at each end.

It will be noted that in the figure the join of side crown comes at the back; this is optional; the pattern must be taken to fit all round, and cut down at the least conspicuous part, in a straight line from crown top to headline, but the *front* must be *marked*, and the pattern so placed that this comes on the bias line. It is clearly shown in the figure how the bias line runs directly through from middle front to back in each part of the pattern.

There are deviations from this rule. In Fig. 3 it will be seen that the bias lines are so placed that a straight line runs along the one side of join at the back, and directly through the middle front; joins fit smoother the more on the straight they can be managed, and the one straight line will hold the other, which is on a slight angle, in sewing; this last must be held *towards you,* when slipstitching.

Dome crowns are covered by stretching over as tightly as possible a piece of the material, the bias line running exactly from back to front; they will stand a lot of stretching and coaxing, and, unless very deep, almost every little wrinkle can be worked out; the material is, of course, pinned in place to the muslin bind, and, when perfectly stretched, sewn with a long stitch on one side and a tiny back stitch on the other; or cut a little longer, turned up inside crown, and sewn to the crinoline bind; but if they are very deep, it is best to cover only the top thus, and finish the sides with folds or in some other way.

44

Eccentric Frames

In covering mushroom frames it must be remembered that the edge line is usually of less circumference than that part of the frame that "bulges"; hence a tight, smooth fit can only be obtained by fitting the *edge* and headline, and *stretching* the material around over the curve. This applies equally to silk and velvet. Also in covering mushroom frames the under side must be done first, and the facing, either plain or full, held in place by invisible stitches on the material and long ones on the reverse. In the same way all curved brims must be treated, so that the covering will cling to the frame.

So many shapes have curves that make it impossible to cut the pattern without a join; let this be made to come where it will show least, and if possible be hidden by trimming. As this depends so much on the shape and design of the moment, no rule can be given, but silk or velvet should be neatly stitched, the seams opened and the piece replaced on the frame, but sheer materials are best merely lapped over. (See "Making Joins.")

Making the Hat

As before said, the rule is to put the upper brim covering on first, except in frames that curve like a mushroom. The pieces should be marked with cross pins corresponding to the marks on the pattern before removing this, then, when placed on the frame, mark to mark, the pieces will fit. Smooth out with the flat hand from the headline out, taking care, however, to smooth at the *straight* of the goods, never at the bias, or the piece will be stretched and the fit ruined. Now pin at back, front, and sides at the edge, then between these pins, and again between. Being sure that the piece is smooth as hands can make it, turn it over the edge and pin it to the muslin bind, pins *head down;* but if the margin has stretched to more than the ½ inch, pare it more; it may be less, but must not be more. Having pinned it all round, sew the turning to the muslin

45

bind with a large shallow "cat-stitch." (See Fig. 4.) Many milliners use a long stitch with a very short "pick-up" stitch, passing the needle straight towards the edge. The snipped margin that turns up against the crown need not be sewn now.

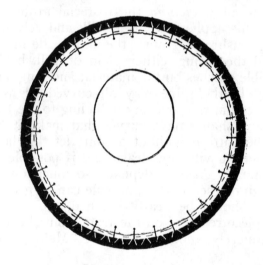

FIG. 4—UPPER VELVET COVERING STRETCHED ON BRIM, EDGE TURNED OVER, PINNED TO MUSLIN BIND, AND "CAT-STITCHED" TO THIS

Next the under facing is put on, laid mark to mark, and pinned back, front, and sides to the edge, then between as before, and smoothed out till not a wrinkle is left; then trim off the margin to one-third of an inch, turn this in so both edges are level, and pin, with the tiny English or fine steel pins, *heads up*. This is so the pin marks shall not mark the velvet.

This facing, *held towards* you, is now welded to the other by a short "slip-stitch" just inside the two edges. (See Fig. 5.)

Take up a fraction, not more than one-sixteenth of an inch, just inside the turn of the *lower* facing, passing the point of the needle at once into the upper facing, where you pick up as small a bit; draw up the thread close; now, in repeating for the next stitch, put the needle in right opposite to where you last brought it out; thus you have a slanting and perpendicular stitch alternately, which will close the two edges effectually. Drop out the pins one ahead as you work, and hold edge firmly with finger and thumb of left hand, so it cannot slip and cause fullness or twists. It is well to hold a cutting of velvet over the edge under finger and thumb, so that the pressure may not mar the velvet.

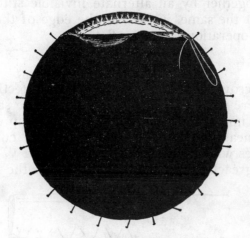

FIG. 5—UNDER VELVET FACING PINNED ON AND "SLIPSTITCHED"

Uncut Velvet

In using "uncut" velvet, the direction of the ribs must be considered in place of the pile of ordinary velvet; the same is the case with corded or even gros-grain silks; broadcloth has a shine equal to mirror velvet.

Making Joins

There are three ways of making joins in brims; the nature of material and shape must decide which to use. In a firm material the two edges may be pinned together so that one can trim them to a ½ inch, then the brim covering partly loosened and the join made (closely back-stitched) on the wrong side, flattened out, and re-laid in place. In some shapes it is not safe to do this; then the bias side of the join is laid in place on the frame, and the straight side turned in and laid over it, pinned securely and slip-stitched down.

The third method is the "woven" join; in this both edges of join are best on the bias or nearly so; both are turned under so the edges just meet, and are slip-stitched closely together by an alternate invisible stitch in each edge, just the same, in fact, as the edge of the hat, only that this operation is on the flat.

Covering the Crowns

For a crown the sides of which are perfectly straight, i. e., where the circumference of top is the same as the headline, no pattern is needed, as a bias strip will stretch round; measure the depth of crown, and cut the strip two inches wider; you need one inch for a ½-inch turning along each edge, and it will stretch the other inch

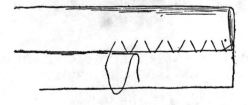

FIG. 6—EDGE OF VELVET "CAT-STITCHED" DOWN

narrower. Turn the edges over and "cat-stitch" them down as shown in Fig. 6. To do this so no stitch shows on the right side, the upper stitch is taken only in the *overturned* part of material, taking care not to catch the under side; the lower stitch is just *one thread* of the *back* of the material taken up; the stitches should be of equal size and depth, and not pulled too tight, or they will pucker the web on the right side.

48

The crown top may be cut out first with a sufficient margin, or a corner cutting stretched on, taking care to get it on the right bias and shading. Pin to the bind, then sew down, so there is not a bit of fullness around the edge; sew half or a third of an inch below the edge in an even line of stiches, ½ inch long on the *right* side, with a tiny back stitch inside the crown; trim off all material below the line of stiches. Now stretch on the bias strip, letting the one edge come level with top of crown; the lower neatens the snipped margin of the upper brim which runs up against the crown. (See Fig. 7.) Let the join of the side crown

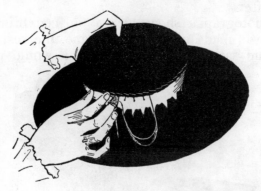

FIG. 7—SEWING COVERING ON TOP OF CROWN.
SHOWING FINISHED BRIM

come where the trimming will cover it, turn one end in over the other, and slip-stitch down; it needs no other sewing.

Sloping crowns must be cut to pattern and snugly fitted; if the tip is smaller than the base, the margin must be snipped round, so that it will turn over flat and not ride up; if the base is the smaller circle, then this is snipped; in either case it is well to cut a piece of the thin crinoline muslin to the *exact* pattern; turn the edges over this and "cat-stitch" them to the muslin; then, if the fit is as snug as it should be, it will not need slip-stitching round the edge of crown in a "bell"

49

shape, as the muslin will support it; a sugar loaf crown
—one with tip smaller than base—must be so snugly
fitted that it needs only the join slip-stitching the same
as a straight crown. The side must come level with
top in either case. In thin materials cut the crinoline a
little larger than patterns and turn over with the outer
covering.

Finishing Edges

There are, of course, various other ways of finishing
edges. One is a bind; in this case the velvet is cut without an edge margin, this being just top sewn to the
muslin bind, and the bias velvet bind, wide or narrow,
put on after.

The photographs show such a finished brim, but as
the hat was made over a wire frame, the result is not
as flat and satisfactorily perfect, as it would prove on

FIG. 8

one of stiff fine cape net, buckram or sparterie. (Fig.
7.) In this case the bind was 1 inch wide when finished on either side, and allowing the stretching necessary to ensure the *inner* circles having *no fullness,* the
bind was cut 4 inches wide.

Covering Wire Frames

If a wire frame is to be covered plain with velvet
or silk, it must be very perfectly covered under and
over with crinoline cut to pattern, then the edge bound;
if silk is to be used the layer of sheet wadding will be
necessary.

Toques and turbans have a bias stripe of crinoline stretched around the outside of the brim, the edge turned over the edge wire and *basted* on below it; slits are cut up from the lower edge, and lapped to fit, or wedges cut out, so the covering is smooth and light as possible.

The crown, if a dome is covered with one piece, stretched over, slits cut up from the headline towards the top, and lapped to fit, and sewn to the crinoline that turns up inside the crown from the brim covering.

If the crown is a flat top shape, the side is first covered with a bias strip stretched around, or if very

FIG. 9

sloping this must be cut to shape; then the tip is put on, cut with a ½-inch margin, which is snipped, turned over on to the side band, the snips lapped and sewn to side band with a ½-inch long stitch.

The foregoing is intended for solid coverings only; when sheer effects are desired, the frames are covered with tulle, mousseline de soie, or tarlatan, or even Brussels net, when lace motifs are to be appliqued on.

Plain Covering

To plain cover a wire frame with tulle, at least four layers should be used on each side of the brim, and six or eight over the crown. If colored, the frame must match; a charming idea is to have silver or gold wire frames for white or very delicate colored tulle hats.

Mousseline de soie and chiffon are used in the same way, two layers on each side are enough of these; and of crêpe de chine only one layer is needed on each side. Crêpe Francaise is rarely used to make a hat, being employed merely as a frame covering, a foundation for some better material to go over; it comes in all colors, is quite wide, and only twenty or twenty-five cents the yard. Tarlatan is also used, but is not suitable for any purpose that will allow it to show. It comes in all colors, is very wide and inexpensive.

An excellent quality of tulle comes at twenty-five cents the yard, anything cheaper is unsuited for either plain covering or shirring.

To cover frames take a correct pattern in paper or thin interlining muslin; measure widest diameter across, fold a square of this diameter of as many layers of the material as are required, pin together firmly, pin pattern on (back and front on a *bias* line) and cut with a one-half inch turning at edge, and one inch at headline, which must be snipped in to headline. Cut upper and under sets of layers separately and place upper set on brim first, turn edge over wire and run a thread around under the wire; place under coverings in place, turn edge over wire and run; this will be covered by the bind. Pin together and run round the two sets of facings just above the headwire.

Crowns are best covered in one piece,—from two to six-ply according to material;—dome crowns must be stretched as smooth as possible, unless they are treated in some artistic way; plain low crowns may have the circular piece drawn down in tiny plaits to the head line, or a draped or "Tam" crown may cover the frame. If it is a high crown the top may be plain, and the sides done in flat folds, or some other pretty way.

52

LESSON IV

CUTTING MATERIALS — MAKING BINDS AND FOLDS

To Get the True Bias

THE rule to get a true bias is: Fold the material over so the selvedge comes in line with the cut end, or cross web; but in some materials it makes a difference which corner is folded over; one way will

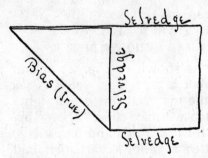

FIG. I

HOW TO GET A TRUE BIAS

give a rich, even effect, in the other it will split the pile or surface grain; this must be tested. (See Fig. 1.) This "true" bias is necessary for all binds and folds.

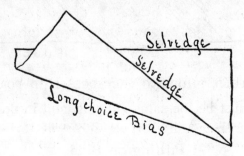

FIG. 2

CHOICE BIAS A

But one may need for a draping or other trimming a bias piece without a join; in this case we cut a "long

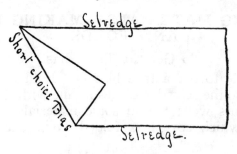

FIG. 3
CHOICE BIAS B

choice bias," as shown in Fig. 2; or our piece may be too small to cut a true bias, yet it is necessary or best not to have the material on the straight, as for a bow-knot, etc.; then we may cut a "short" bias, as in Fig. 3.

In cutting for bias folds and binds it is very necessary to be accurate; a tailor's yardstick laid down on the wrong side and the line chalk-marked will ensure this.

All joins must be along the selvedges or on the straight side of the web in the opposite direction, and

FIG. 4
CUT BIAS FOLD, SHOWING SELVEDGES LAID FOR JOINING

all grain must be the same at joins, and in velvet shade the same way. A join *across* the bias is incorrect.

Putting on Binds

There are three kinds of binds, the narrow, wide, and full bind.

54

The narrow bind is treated thus: Cut the strips, one or two, according to circumference of hat, double the width *through the bias* as the desired width of bind *when finished*. Cut off the selvedges and join (see Fig. 4), taking care the two strips shade the same way; one end is right, the other will be wrong; join with a close back-stitch, with a ⅓-inch margin, taking care to get the edges level at join; press flat with the thimble. Now pin one end of the strip on edge of brim, stretch firmly round till the pinned end is reached, mark with pin, take off hat, lay flat on table, fold over so the end meets the pin, and *cut off in line with the selvedge end;* join these ends, and press flat.

Now pin the bind wrong side up on upper side of brim near the edge; take care to have all even, or there

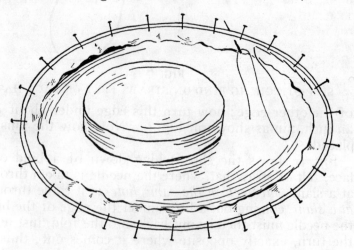

EIG. 5—NARROW BIND PINNED ON EDGE
READY FOR SEWING

will be too much "stretch" at one place and too much fullness at another (see Fig. 5); when correctly pinned (dividing in quarters is a safe plan) sew along with a stitch similar to that used to sew on tip of crown, *i. e.,* a long stitch on the material and a short backstitch underneath; the turning allowed need not be more than a ¼ inch, but this must be kept at an even distance from the edge. Now press both thumbs under the sewn edge and snap sharply over; this prevents the stretching

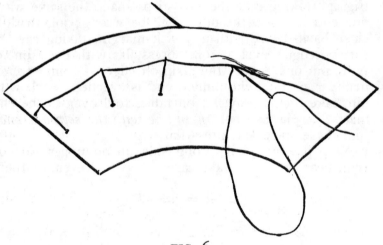

FIG. 6

SLIP-STITCHING BIND ON STRAW, FELT OR LACE HAT

of the other edge; now turn this edge under about ⅓ of an inch, pin as shown in Fig. 6. Note how the pins are placed.

Fig. 6 shows the slipstitching down of a bind on a lace, felt or straw hat, where the needle is taken through at a slant, *put back in the same hole* as it came through, *at a slant,* coming out a little under the edge of the bind; the needle must then be put back into the fold, just under the turn, exactly opposite where it comes out; thus we get the requisite short straight stitch and longer slanting stitch.

The wide bind is cut by the same rule; thus, if we wish a bind showing one inch on each side when finished, it is cut 4 inches *through the bias;* if the material is very stretchy or ravelly, it must be cut from 1 to 2 inches wider. The strips are then joined, stretched on *along the middle,* so that there is the least possible fullness left along the cut edges, then marked and joined the same as the narrow bind; but when done it is slipped on the hat, the middle along the edge, so both cut edges come even, half on either side. Now the edges are turned under, both as you proceed; *i. e.,* not first one and then the other, taking care to keep them even (the fingers can feel this), and pin as directed in Fig. 6; the turning under should be generous, as it easily works out.

In a lace, felt, or straw hat both sides are slip-stitched at the same time with one line of stitches, the short slip-stitch being taken alternately under and over the brim, with the short straight stitch, the needle passing along inside the edge for not more than ⅛ of an inch, and passing through to the other side on a short slant, then repeat.

If, however, the bind is put on a velvet or silk hat, or any other solid material, each side is separately slip-stitched; hold the hat so the edge of bind to be sewn is downward towards you (see Fig. 7) and pass the needle

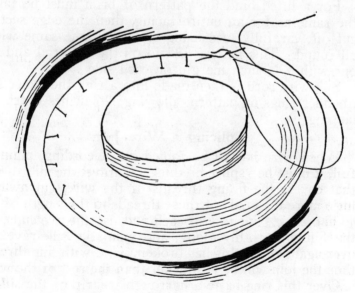

FIG. 7—SLIPSTITCHING BIND ON VELVET HAT

⅛ of an inch inside edge of fold, pick up 1/16 of an inch of material of brim under edge of fold, pass needle back into fold opposite where it comes out, and repeat, drawing the thread straight, but not too tight, as this will cause little waves where the stitches are, though these may not show.

In putting binds on sheer hats, such as tulle, net, lace, etc., the wide bind is best, and may be put on and slip-stitched in same way as a felt hat. If a narrow bind only is desired, it can be put on the same as before directed, but the turnover must be no wider than the other side, and be slip-stitched against it, so no stitches show.

The widest bind that is safe to put on in strip form is 1¾ inches; if desired wider than this, the edge must be *cut to shape,* and is best set on with a wire cording. Wire cording may also be used to finish a bias bind.

Fitted Bind

For a fitted bind the pattern of brim must be taken the same as for an entire facing, then the edge section cut off, carefully measuring to have it the same width all round. This pattern is laid on the material and cut out with a ½-inch margin on each side.

Silk wire cord is then made into a ring the exact size of inner rings of pattern, allowing 1½ inches extra for lapping.

Splicing a Wire Join

When wire has to be joined for a cording, plain or full, it must be "spliced," thus: Unravel the silk thread that covers the filling threads of the wire, cut away a little more than half of these threads to the length of the join, *i. e.,* 1½ inches, on each end, lap the two ends, lay the filling smoothly along, and wind the silk ravelling over again, or, if this has broken, wind with fine thread; thus the join will be no thicker than the rest of the wire.

Over this ring baste a narrow bias strip of the silk or velvet, lay it in place on the brim, pin and baste on, *not* taking any stitches through; now pin on the bind at a few places, allowing ½ an inch to come beyond edge of brim; the other edge should project ½ an inch beyond the wire cord, and be snipped all round, so it will turn under quite flat; turn under, pin all round as shown in Fig. 6, and slip-stitch down close against the cord. The edge that turns over edge of brim should have been secured by a few pins; now pin as directed for a regular covering, and cat-stitch down.

If an under bind is to be put on the same as the upper, a wire cord may now be set around the *edge,* and the edge of bind slip-stitched to this, the inner circle being treated the same as above; but the two edges can be slip-stitched together without the cord.

Sectional Facing

Sometimes one leaves the edge of a straw, leghorn, or felt untrimmed, and puts a band of velvet or silk on a section of the brim. In this case such section is cut out of the entire pattern, then cut out in fine cape net, this carefully wired around both edges, as directed in the Lesson on Frames. The velvet is cut ½ inch larger around each edge, pinned on the net foundation and cat-stitched thereto, not allowing a stitch to show on the right side. This sectional facing is then pinned in place on the brim and slip-stitched down.

If the facing is to come from the headsize out part way on the brim, only the edge is wired as before directed, and 1 inch turning allowed at the headsize, both in net and velvet, which is snipped and turned up, being invisibly secured inside the crown and neatened by the headlining.

Full Binds are treated in the Lesson on Shirring.

Folds

Still another way to treat the edges of hats is to baste a bias strip around, well stretched over the edge wire,

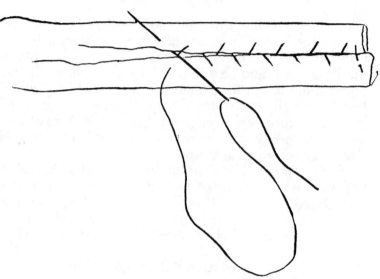

FIG. 8—LACING OR BALL STITCH

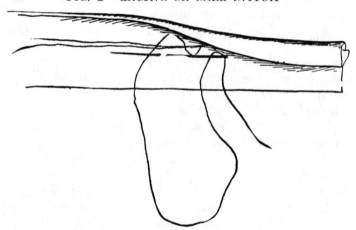

FIG. 9—SLIP-STITCHING "FRENCH" FOLD

then neaten these edges by slip-stitching a fold over, either a plain fold (see Fig. 8) or a "French" or "milliner's" fold (see Fig. 9).

A plain fold is made by cutting a narrow bias strip of velvet, silk, or other material, and joining the edges

as shown in Fig. 8. A milliner's fold is cut wider, the
edges laid together the same as before, but the upper
part turned over again as in a hem, and this "slip" or
blind-stitched down on the lower half, taking up alternately 1/16 of an inch above and below, but keeping all
stitches *under* the turnover (see Fig. 9). It is a help
to beginners to make the fold first the same as a plain
fold (turning up ⅔ and down ⅓), then turning over and
slip-stitching.

Care must be taken to keep the fold even, and a stitch
taken *through* will cause twisting.

Measures for length of folds are taken the same as
for binds, so that joins can be made first.

In a transparent hat it is essential that the bind be
the same width on both sides; in this way the stitches
are hidden, and nothing heavier than 100 thread should
be used; in fact, 200 is best.

Binds of an inch or over on each side are prepared
in the same way, but the joins must be made first, and
silk has the wadding basted on flat, *i. e.*, not made into a
fold. The piece is then stretched at its middle line over
edge of frame; the cut edges must have no fullness, and
are turned under so they are even on both sides; these
are then slipstitched with *one line* of stitches, under and
over at the same time.

Narrow folds of tulle or silk are often set over the
round wires, under and over the brim and round the
crown; these may be plain or French folds; or thick
satin cord wire is covered with a narrow strip of bias
silk or velvet sewn on in an even line, and this slip-
stitched round, the stitches against the hat. Bias French
folds of tulle are hard to make, but practice will conquer
the difficulty; it is best to pin and baste the several
layers together, then fold and pin, always having the
pins heads *down*.

LESSON V

SHIRRINGS AND FOLDS

The Frame and Covering

OF course shirred and tucked velvet or silk can be and often is used over solid frames, but it is not best, and should be avoided if possible; good firm cape net, well braced, is good, but a firm wire frame covered smoothly with thinnest crinoline muslin is of all things the best. In some cases the crinoline covering even may be dispensed with; that depends entirely on the nature of the work, if or not it is needed to secure any part of the tucking or shirring to, as this is the only reason for covering the frame first. In using silk, the under-covering may be even lighter, such as cheap tarlatan.

In all things the worker must use forethought and common sense; the easiest way that will yield the best results is the right way. If the frame is not covered first it will be found of great help to put a double bias band of crinoline one-inch or more wide around the inside of the crown at the headline; it should be sewn to the headwire with a longish buttonhole stitch. This makes a firm foundation to which to sew both brim and crown work, and later the trimming.

To Measure and Cut the Velvet

To measure for the piece required first decide if the upper and under, or outer and inner brims are to be all in one piece. In small hats, toques and similar shapes, the material is frequently in one from the outer headline to the headsize inside the crown; but in large flat shapes this is very rarely the case, the under brim being more usually faced with folds or shirrings of a sheer material. In either case measure the widest part of brim, add to this the necessary turning at headline and edge, then add for whatever tucks you intend putting in and still one inch more for "making." This last

62

inch is added even if the work is flat shirrings only; and this measure is taken *through the bias,* not along the selvedge. To calculate the length piece you need, measure along the edge wire, add half as much again for velvet, or a little more, and double the measure for silk. Now measure your bias material from selvedge to selvedge, and you can easily find how many times that measure you will need to make the strip for the shirred piece.

Importance of Shading and Joins

In cutting have a care that all your pieces have the same slant at the selvedges or they will not join right; cut off the selvedges, and join all the pieces so they form a ring, taking care that all *shade the same way,* one end of each strip will shade right, the other end wrong (see Fig. 1 showing joined piece); join as for a fold or bind with close backstitch, or better still, baste carefully and stitch on machine.

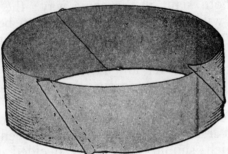

FIG. 1—SHOWING JOINED BREADTHS

If wires are to be inserted, all seams must be turned *one* way, and wires pushed in in the same direction, if pushed in *against* the join they will catch. But if it is just shirrings or tucks the seams are flattened out the same as for binds.

Measuring and Marking for Shirrings

The next step is to mark off for the work to be put in. In flat shirrings this is easily done on the wrong

63

side. An effective and easy way is to make "blind" shirrings, that is, instead of flat runners, to fold over the material at the desired line, and "whip" the shirring in (Fig. 2); it gives a rather richer effect and shows no stitches on the right side.

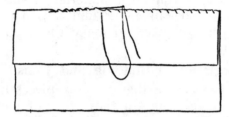

FIG. 2—"WHIPPED" FLAT SHIRRING

To return for a moment to the joining; in the case of a toque where the brim is not carried around the back, the strip is left open at one join but usually one or both ends will need a bit joined on to make both straight, or both slant in the same way; the shape of brim at back will indicate which will go on best.

The number of shirrings and the spaces between are matters for the designer to decide, but whatever is done must be *accurate,* and having decided on this, cut notches in a card to measure by; never do things carelessly.

If tucks are to be made use the same method, decide on the depth of the tucks, the spaces between, and the number (which should have been decided on when cutting the strips); and with the notched card, measure off and pin, and if necessary baste all lines. Having folded the material over for the tuck, pin it with the pins *across* the work (Fig. 3); then, if you have not an even eye, indicate the line to be shirred with a fine basting thread accurately measured.

All runners must be kept perfectly flat until the entire work is done, therefore cut your threads—which should be strong twist silk for velvet, and machine twist for silk—a little longer than the piece to be shirred, bringing all joins at the same place, if the piece is long, it makes the drawing up easier to divide the work in half, or even quarters.

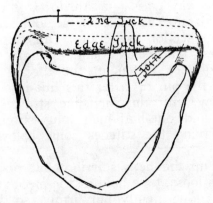

FIG. 3—TUCK PINNED FOR SHIRRING,
EDGE TUCK RUN

The quantities given are the usual rule, but if very fluffy edge tucks are desired, more is to be allowed, but never more than double the length of velvet or three times of *thin* silk. (See Fig. 4.)

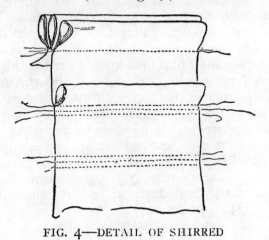

FIG. 4—DETAIL OF SHIRRED
FACING WITH TUCKS

To Put on Brim Piece

Having run all shirrings and tucks required for brim, divide the piece in eight equal parts, divide the edge of frame in same way (it is not safe to trust to the eight cross wires of frame as these are seldom accurately divided), and pin section to section. Draw up the thread at the *edge* first, pin evenly round, dividing the fullness as you pin, do not fasten off the threads, but twist lightly round the pin till after this line is sewn fast to the edge. Sew with tiny invisible stitches along the shirred line, and one-half inch long stitches on the under side, having the stitches come below the edge wire.

Now draw up the next shirrings but not too tight, leave the ends loose, take hold of the piece at the head-line and pull down gently but firmly, so that all the little flutes run in an even line from edge to head. Hold the edge of hat against you, inside of crown uppermost, and working from *right* to *left* run a shirring thread in the piece *just inside* the headline, guiding the work with fingers and thumb of left hand; draw this up to fit, and sew inch long stitches inside head and small back stitches outside, if the shirring is a facing; if it is an upper brim do the same around outside base of crown. Now even the fullness of the other shirrings of tucks, and fasten off all ends. This is best done by tying each two ends in a firm knot, then threading each end into a long needle, and passing the thread under the work an inch or two, and cutting close off, it will work inside, and, being long, is not likely to loosen. The intermediate shirring needs no securing to the frame, except in the case of curved frames, where the work must be attached by tiny stitches on the right side and long ones on the reverse. In mushroom shapes the under side must be done first, and in sailors the upper is the first to be set on.

The Double Edge Frill

Some milliners lay two tucks and use only one runner, passing the needle through the four thicknesses of material. We do not approve of this; in the first place it is so thick that it is impossible to make a neat runner, and in the second, the two tucks cling so closely together that the desired effect is lost. Let the tucks be laid and run separately, but with not more than one-sixteenth of an inch space between the two runners. (See Fig. 4.)

Shirring Velvet and Silk for Wire Casings

Supposing the hat is to be of silk on both sides, cut your strips double the widest measure from headline to edge, plus any edge tucks; fold this (after joining) through the middle, wrong side out, baste the two thicknesses together, a one-fourth inch from the folded line. Now fold a tuck of the required depth over on each side, so the right side comes outside; be sure they are even, pin carefully with pins *across*, not *along* the tucks, and run a shirring thread through the four thicknesses along the basted line, then run a second just below the inner folded edge through the two thicknesses of brim. In this instance the running of the first thread through the four layers can hardly be avoided, as the one casing must hold the tucks, unless they are made to come one on each side of the edge wire, when a separate casing must be run below them, which means four runners instead of two.

Now the spaces are marked off the same as for single faced shirring, the two layers of material carefully pinned and, if necessary, basted together and the shirrings put in in sets of two, with from one-eighth to one-fourth of an inch space between for the wires, and from one to one and one-half inches space between each casing; these must be just wide enough to take the wires nicely, if too narrow the wire will not go in, if too wide, it will look clumsy. Be sure to keep the entire work flat till all is done. In this work it is important that the seams ot joins all turn one way.

If tucks are desired on the upper brim, and the under one is plain shirring, allow extra for these in measuring, and instead of folding the piece through the middle, fold it at the required brim depth, plus one edge tuck, thus leaving the surplus for additional tucks on one side only. Proceed as before directed for edge tucks, then put in first runner of second casing, but before putting in the second runner, pick up, pin and run a tuck, having the shirring line come close against, *but not touching,* the first runner; now put second runner of casing below tuck runner; on the upper or tuck side three lines of shirring are seen, but on the under side are only the two forming the wire casing. (See Fig. 4.)

How to Put In the Wires

"How do I get the wires in?" is the question of the novice, and it is a most important one. In shirring, be it single or double, three or four inches of the casings and tucks must be left unrun at the back or least conspicuous part of the brim; here the wires are run in, beginning at the edge wire, which must be cut three inches longer than intended measure and the two ends pushed across each other and firmly joined. This is easiest done by a buttonhole stitch around the two wires, beginning and ending with a firm tie knot, then finish the runners across the join, fulling up as you go because it is almost impossible to push fullness over the joined wires. The second wire, then the others in succession are put in in the same way, the head wire being the last. To run in the wires, turn a bit over and pinch it close with the pliers so that it will not catch in the material; thick wire that cannot be turned over, must be firmly twisted over at the end, so it will not ravel.

If a perfectly flat brim is desired the length of the wires can be easily ascertained by laying the work flat on the table and drawing up till the flutes run stretched from the edge in; but if a curved brim is desired, a buckram frame should be used as a mold to work over; only an expert can shape her wires to artistic lines in eccentric shapes. After the wires are in, draw up and fasten off all threads as before directed.

If it is desired to have a sheer underfacing separately shirred or of folds, use a thin silk or muslin for the reverse of the shirrings, then make and slipstitch the facing on around the edge, *after* the crown has been set on, then carry the headline, ravelled edge up, inside the crown, and finish with the head lining. Wires are not necessary in such underfacings but cross braces are frequently put in on velvet brims to prevent them sagging.

If soft brims are desired, use in place of wire "shirring cord," which is very stiff but can be cut with the scissors; feather-bone reeds are also used.

These methods of shirring are more especially used in children's millinery.

Crowns

Crowns may be made in several ways. They can, of course, be shirred with casings and drawn to shape the same as the brim, using silk or muslin underneath, in which case they will need a support of cross wires buttonholed in after the round wires have been drawn to the required size and shape. But it is easier and more practical to form the crown shape in wire, cover it with thin crinoline and shirr or tuck single ply material to harmonize with the brim. This may be of bias or straight material, or it may be, as in the case of a "Tam" or shirred "mob" crown, made from a round piece three times the diameter of the crown top. From the middle of this cut an even round the size of the crown top, run a shirring thread around this edge, a one-fourth inch in; turn under the outer edge and run a narrow tuck, put in three or four shirrings above this one, with a one-half inch between each. One inch from the other edge runner put in another shirring, and a couple more if the crown is to be flat on top. Draw the rough edge shirring up tight so the ravellings come on the wrong side, sew firmly and flatten out, sew invisibly on center of crown, draw up edge tuck, even the fullness, pin and sew around headline; this neatens the rough finish of brim shirring. Now draw up the other threads to shape and place, pass ends inside crown and fasten off.

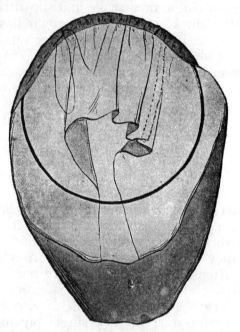

FIG. 5
SHIRRING EDGE OVER WIRE RING

The crown made from bias strips is finished in the same way, but as there is more fullness to dispose of, cannot well be drawn to a center on crown; draw as close as it will allow and finish with a flat button or bit of separate shirring; or sew a flat piece on top of crown and finish top edge on a wire cord as shown in Fig. 5.

Shirred Plaques

Entire plaques can be shirred in this way, either drawing a hole cut in middle of round to a center, or sewing a plain flat round on the middle of a net foundation, and gathering the piece on a wire around this central disk.

Shirring On Cord

The same idea is shown in Fig. 6, a shirred plateau of velvet, done over thick cords. This was made over a firm cape net foundation, well braced, the deep bandeau forming the crown. Three bias lengths of velvet were used, reaching from the headsize — under edge of bandeau — to the central ring on top, puffing easily over the edge; of course, in measuring for width of breadths this has to be allowed for, also the cordings,

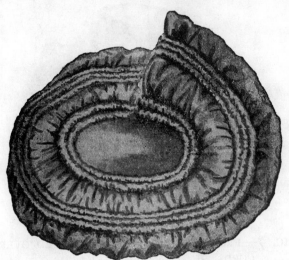

FIG. 6
VELVET HAT SHIRRED OVER CORDS

which is one inch to each, beside turnings at headsize, and last ring; a little puffiness between the two sets of cords, and an extra inch for the "making" of underbrim, although this was done in flat shirrings. After joining and opening the seams, the inner cord was done first, holding the material firmly around it, and running under so as not to catch the cord, but leaving both cord and

71

shirring thread a little longer than the material. The second cord is laid in as close as possible to the first, shirred in in the same way, bringing the joins and ends at the same place and leaving three inches unrun as directed for the wire casings.

Now we measure off one inch, and if necessary baste the line and put in the set of three cords. Now the material must be placed on the foundation to ascertain just where the first set of three flat shirrings is to go on under brim, probably four to five inches from the last cord; then a space of one inch and a couple more shirrings, and a last one to gather all into the headsize.

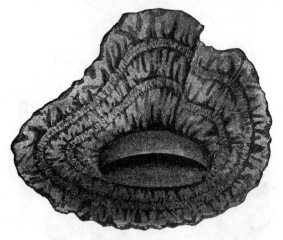

FIG. 7—FRONT VIEW OF HAT SHIRRED OVER CORDS, SHOWING FLAT SHIRRING

Having sewn a flat piece on top middle of foundation, the first cord is drawn up, cut to size, the ends lapped and tightly wound round; if very thick and firm, cut away half of each end, so that when lapped the join will be no larger than the rest of the cord; this is called "splicing," and is also done with the thick covered wire used in Figs. 5 and 8. Pin this cording in place, and draw up the thread, but do not fasten off till all is done. Now draw up and fasten off the other cords, pinning and arranging as the work proceeds. The instruction of dividing into eighths given previously applies here, and makes the work of equalizing the fullness much easier. It is not quite easy to push the fullness over the cords, but firm fingering does it.

Only the first, third and last rows of cording are sewn to foundation, the first with one-half inch long stitches on wrong side, invisible ones among the shirring; the other two may have longer stitches on the reverse.

Next the first set of under shirrings are drawn up and attached *invisibly* in such a way as to ensure the edge puff retaining its effect. (Fig. 7.) Now the lower shirrings; last the headline is drawn up and secured; then the bandeau, previously covered, is sewn on, and a headlining finishes the hat. The curve shown was bent in after the hat was made, and gave it a droop on the right side. The only trimming consisted of two plumes posed on the underbrim, where it turned up, and a handsome ornament outside.

Toques are handsome shirred in this way; it is very

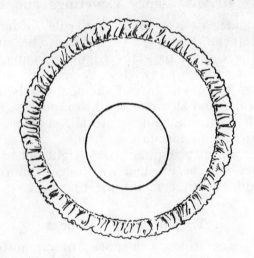

FIG. 8

FULL EDGE SHIRRED OVER WIRE CORD

effective for crape and crêpe de chine; and big rosettes with corded edges are handsome.

Also this cording may be done in flat tucks; *i. e.,* the velvet finely run over the cords and *not fulled up.*

Returning to the wire cording, this is a good method of finishing full edges on either straw, felt, velvet, or silk hats, and equally so for crape. The strip is gathered along, one edge divided into eighths, the same with the hat, and sections pinned to sections, the thread drawn up, and the bind sewn on the brim, rough edge *towards* the edge, and, of course, wrong side up. Now cut a cord or cable wire ring the size required, ravel the ends and "splice," turn the other edge of the bind over the wire, shirr along, fulling, and drawing up the thread; hold the work on the side of brim where the cording is to go, as you cannot slip it over after it is done.

To sew to hat, use an invisible stitch among the fullness and a longer one underneath. (See Figs. 5 and 8.)

Sheer Materials, Fancy Coverings and Facings

Sheer materials are used as a rule in fancy ways, shirrings, tucks, plaitings, or folds. The simplest of these is the shirred or gathered underfacing, which is suitable for either a straw, felt, velvet, silk, or lace hat; next comes a tucked shirred facing. Folds are put in in three ways, and as a rule the brim must be first faced plain with some matching material, such as thin silk, crêpe Française or tarlatan.

In a straw the facing may come right out to the edge, or the edge may be finished with one or more rows of straw braid, the underfacing meeting this.

To Allow for Fullness

Of tulle, four times (or more) of circumference of hat.

Of mousseline de soie, three times of circumference of hat.

74

Sheer chiffon, three times of circumference of hat.
Heavier chiffon, twice circumference of hat.
Crêpe de chine, twice circumference of hat.
Silk, twice circumference of hat.

Formerly such materials as tulle or maline, mousseline de soie, crêpe lisse, crêpe Française, or aerophane, crêpe de chine, chiffon, Liberty gauze, silk blond (so called from the blond hair formerly used in its manufacture), Brussels net, besides the various veilings and laces, were used only in summer wear, but these are now employed equally for winter wear, the dressy evening and "restaurant" hats being as airy in design as the most dainty summer chapeaux.

Tulle, which is the lightest of these fabrics, has not 'the softening effect to the face as have some of the other materials; hence it needs making up with special care to give the effect which in itself it lacks. Plain covered white tulle hats are like a piece of marble against the face; done in soft folds or fluffy puffings and shirrings it can be made becoming, but its immense popularity is due to its judicious use as a setting for soft trimmings such as feathers, and dainty color effects in flowers or

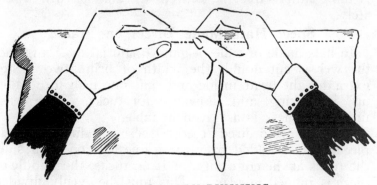

FIG. 9— FLY RUNNING

other garnitures; a touch of velvet or fur in winter gives a touch of real fascination to this beautiful material.

The beauty of tucks and shirring depends on their

being evenly spaced and finely run, and it is safest to mark the first line by measurement and pins. It is best to make all joins before beginning to shirr, but in very long lengths of tulle it is permissible to keep the work flat, and fold the ends neatly in when putting the piece on the hat.

The best way to shirr all light goods is by "fly running." (See Fig. 9.) The cut shows how the work is held, but the method is to propel the needle with the thimble and *wave* it back and forth in a quick tiny stitch through the material; when mastered this is a very neat and swift method.

In putting on a facing with a cluster of tucks at the edge, it is best to draw up the threads and pin in place, twisting the threads around a pin as one does in plain sewing gathers, for the reason that in sewing on a little more is often taken up, necessitating the letting out of the draw threads.

A cluster of deep edge tucks of tulle may be laid and pinned, then secured with one runner, but in silk, crêpe de chine, or chiffon, they must be run singly, leaving a one-sixteenth of an inch only between. (See Fig. 4.) A more fluffy effect is secured by running each separately.

Sheer Hats Made Direct on Frame

In hats made of tulle or gauzy material over a frame, the web is cut double the width of brim, two inches extra for the head inside and out, one inch for "take-up" in making, and allowance for tucks. The measure for fullness is as given in table.

If tucks are desired at edge these are first run, the piece is then folded over the frame half on each side, the tucks at the edge wire, or if no tucks, the middle of piece is pinned in place. This must be evenly divided in half back and front, half again each side and again each section halved and *pinned to the brace wires,* as when shirred the work cannot be pulled over these. (Fig. 10.) Now run a shirring thread under the

76

edge wire, forming a casing of upper and under layers, drawing up the thread and evening fullness as work proceeds. Next draw both sides in level flutes down

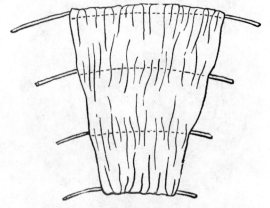

FIG. 10
MOUSSELINE SHIRRED OVER FRAME

taut and shirr together under second, then under third wire, then under head wire. The work may be left

FIG. 11—CORDED MOUSSELINE FACING,
SHIRRED ON FRAME

at that, but many put a second shirring above the wires, which gives the effect of wire casings. Parisian milliners make tulle frames in this way, using them as foundations for lace hats. (See Fig. 11.)

77

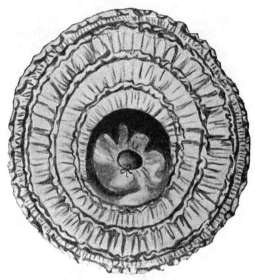

FIG. 12—SHIRRED AND TUCKED FACING IN PLACE

This kind of shirring over frames may be varied in many ways; the shirring may be done on one side only, folding edge of material over edge wire, and encasing

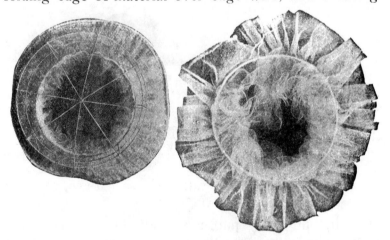

FIG. 13   FIG. 14

TWO METHODS OF SHIRRING

78

each successive circular wire by one row of running;
then the other side is covered with lace, or in any way
desired.

Another way is to have the upper side of silk, and
the under of some sheer material such as chiffon or
crêpe de chine, and shir the two together. It looks
best to finish such edges with cord wire in the silk, as
described above, this being sewn down by an invisible,
slanting slipstitch.

Specimens of Shirred Hats

Figs. 13 and 14 show a shirred tulle hat; the brim
shirred as shown in Fig. 10; the crown is first covered
plain, then a strip shirred on a ring of wire is fitted on
edge of crown, gathered to center, and around headline; the tulle being four times circumference of brim
and crown.

FIG. 15—CHILD'S HAT OF SHIRRED TUCKED
MOUSSELINE DE SOIE, GRADUATED BRIM

Fig. 15 shows a hat of shirred tucks of mousseline
de soie; there are two deep tucks at edge of brim and

crown; three one-half inch tucks on the *upper* brim; the under brim being shirred in rows of whipping stitch, the edge treated as described in Fig. 4.

The crown tucks are a one-quarter inch deep, finished at center by a tuck drawn to a ring over a bit of the mousseline basted on the center top.

When finished the hat was bent to Empire bonnet form and trimmed with ribbon and baby roses.

Graduated Spacings

In Fig. 15 it will be seen that the brim is wider in front than at back; for such a brim the spaces must be *proportionately* graduated. This is done by measurement, the tucks folded and pinned, and a clipped card used to mark off widths of tucks and spacings. If the brim is six inches deep in front and three at back, the spaces between tucks are just double the width in front of that at back, and graduated from one to the other. The same is to be done with the single lines of shirring under the brim, or vice versa.

Facings of Fold

There are three methods of putting in folds of sheer materials. The first is of cut bias folds, run singly round and round on a previously fitted plain foundation of the same material or thing matching silk, and each fold lapping the previous one enough to hide the line of stitches. Such folds are cut bias from two to three

FIG. 16—FACING OF BIAS FOLDS

inches wide, folded double and run on a little full, only enough, however, to insure their being quite flat, not curling over at the folded edge. It is well to pin or baste the necessary quantity, all joins being made first, and the folds run round and round without cutting till the brim is filled in, from edge to headline. (See Fig. 16.)

Another way is to cut off a length of tulle on the straight (other gauzes on the bias) the length of circumference of brim, plus nine inches for every forty, or in that proportion, for ease, not fullness. In tulle it is best to cut the breadth through at the fold; mousseline de soie and chiffon are cut on the bias, about nine inches along the selvedges, which must be joined if necessary to get the requisite lengths, the selvedges cut off, of course. Lay the tulle flat on the table and fold over two inches along one edge; on this fold a tuck one and three-quarters inches deep; fold up as many tucks as the breadth will do, each one-quarter of an inch below the previous one at the top, but all level at the lower part; pin the folds in place as you work, taking out and replacing the pins at a few inches spaces; when all is pinned up, baste *one* thread through all the folds *at the base,* draw up just a little, pin in place on the brim, run down just above the line of basting and when secure draw these out by clipping at short intervals; use 200 thread. Repeat this process with as many breadths as required to fill in the brim.

Sets of deep tucks to fill in spaces between the crown and brim of turbans, etc., are made in this way.

The third method is called a "rucked" facing and is made of the entire breadth of tulle. Cut as before directed, turn the edge over and pin to edge of hat, *push* up the tulle to form one deep fold around the edge, and secure with a "slide" stitch, that is, a long needle is passed under the foundation, and a tiny stitch caught in the tulle at about one and one-half inch spaces. Push

81

up a couple more folds, pin in place, and secure, and so fill in the brim. The extra long milliners' needles known as "straws" are best for this work, or a very fine long darning needle.

Draped effects of tulle or mousseline on brims and crowns are done in the same way as the rucked facings.

If the brim is transparent numerous "tie-stitches" are employed in place of the slide stitch.

Once the milliner understands the nature and possibilities of her materials, a multitude of ideas for their use and best and easiest methods of handling will present themselves; as modes change, so methods change, and the quickest are always best, as much depends on these fragile webs retaining their first freshness and beauty.

LESSON VI

SEWING STRAW HATS

THE manufacturers of straw hats leave less and less to be done in the millinery workroom, producing even the finest hand-made shapes, but even so, it is so often necessary for the designer and maker to make their own hats, that a knowledge of the methods is essential.

As to which method is employed depends on the nature of the braid, the price of the hat, the design, etc., and must be decided as seems best.

It is to be remembered that the directions given for straw braids are equally applicable to winter braids, such as felt, chenille, silk, etc.; but, though all need to be handled with care and neat work, the winter braids need this more especially.

Stitches must never show on the right side, but when an underfacing is used, they may be a little longer than if both sides are to show.

It is rarely necessary to cover a frame with any foundation before sewing on braid, but in the case of very open lacy braids a covering of tulle or net may be desirable; it is also employed when insertion braids are used, so that the edges merely meet instead of lapping; but experience and good judgment will soon teach the milliner when a covering is desirable, remembering never to use it if avoidable.

Edge rows, both with and without frames, may be flat or in form of a bind over the edge wire; in the latter case clasp the wire with the braid, basting the two edges together *within* the edge wire and sew the first flat row to this (see Fig. 8). Only soft braids can be treated thus.

Dampening Braids

Very stiff braids, and very brittle kinds, are best dampened while working, which makes them pliable.

Some will stand a lot of wetting while others may be only rolled in a clean cloth wrung out of clean water. To prepare a very stiff braid for sewing in the morning it is well to leave it rolled in a wet cloth all night. Of course wetted braids dry stiff, and therefore must be most carefully shaped.

The milliner should make herself familiar with the various makes of braids, their names, textures, prices and length of pieces, which she can easily do by visiting wholesale houses.

"Ready-made" or machine made hats have a wire sewn on at the edge which must be carefully removed before trimming, and another sewn on a half inch or more from the edge. If an underfacing or fold is to be

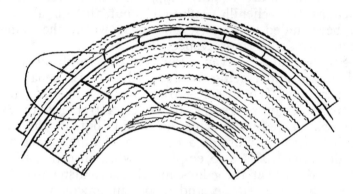

FIG. 1—SEWING WIRE ON STRAW HAT

put on, this wire may be a medium heavy one; but if it is to show, a thick "satin" wire should be used. The first is put on with a three-quarter inch long buttonhole stitch (see Fig. 1); the second with an invisible stitch, taken between the wire and the hat, the needle being passed in a slant through the covering of the wire, through the hat, and back with an invisible stitch (Fig. 2). The ends should lap about an inch, and be twisted over neatly with silk, which should match hat and wire. This method of wiring is also used for hand-made hats without a frame.

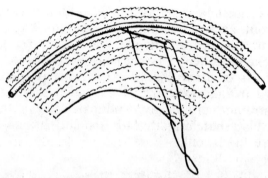

FIG. 2—SLIP-STITCHING SATIN WIRE ON
LEGHORN BRIM, SHOWING SLANT OF
NEEDLE UNDER WIRE

Making a Hat on a Frame

The easiest method to sew a braid hat is, of course, over a frame, which should be wire, *never* buckram; but these must be made sightly under the brim, either by a facing of the same braid, or straw or other web, which is cut to shape; folds or shirrings of some light material, facings of velvet, etc. Sometimes the wires are all twisted over with narrow ribbon or chenille, which is quite decorative.

To sew braid on a frame, begin on one side of the back and sewing from right to left, sew the braid on the edge wire, allowing it to project about half way, sew with a three-quarter inch long stitch (buttonhole is best) over the wire, and an invisible stitch in the braid. If the braid is narrow, cross the end when you get round to it, securing it neatly under the second row, which must lap the first only just enough to secure the scallop of the second to the inner edge of the first row. This inner edge must be drawn in so it forms a flat line conforming to the shape of the hat. This is done by running in a strong thread, or pushing the braid together; sometimes there is a thread woven in the edge by which it can be drawn up. Wide braids must be cut off and neatly turned under at each row.

Each row must be stretched a little at the scallop edge to take out as much fullness as possible at the inner edge, and the nearer the headline, the more it must be stretched. When it is not possible to stretch a braid nor put in a draw thread, the inner edge must be "crowded in" as the next row is sewn on. Dampened braids stretch very easily, and can always be shaped nicely. Use matching thread for dull braids, and for the glossy kinds, silk.

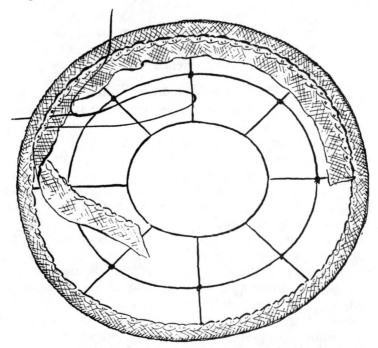

FIG. 3—SHOWING EDGE BOUND WITH FIRST ROW
OF BRAID, AND SECOND ROW BEING SEWN ON

If the brim is the same width all round, the rows should come even to the headline, the last turning up a little against the crown, but if the brim narrows towards the back, graduated part rows are put on around front and sides, one row around the headline neatening all the cut ends, which should turn up against the crown.

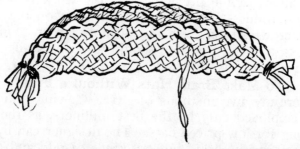

FIG. 4—SLIP-STITCHING TWO BRAIDS TOGETHER,
SHOWING SLANT OF NEEDLE

If the underfacing is of braid, it may be sewn "free"; that is, it is sewn by a pattern the shape of brim, then laid on and the two edge braids "slip" stitched together just above the wire (Fig. 4) and the last row turned up into the headsize and sewn to the crown.

The crown may be sewn in combination with the brim, following the lines of the frame, and finishing with a neat twist-under in the middle; or it can have the top sewn first, beginning at the edge just as the brim was done, then slipstitching the top row of side of crown to the edge row of top, scallop to scallop, and continuing the side with scallops running up; this is nice for bell crowns. (See Fig. 6.)

Another way to sew crowns is from the center out, making a flat button or rosette of the braid, the end

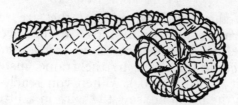

FIG. 5—BEGINNING OF CROWN OR PLAQUE,
SEWING FROM CENTER OUTWARD, SHOW-
ING TURN OF BRAID UNDER SCALLOPS

87

twisted neatly *under,* and each succeeding row stretched at the scallop, so that when the inner edge is sewn *under* the scallops of the previous row, the work is perfectly flat and round. This disk is then sewn on the top of frame crown; it may be a row or more larger, to give the effect of a "bell"; the side should have the scallops running up as before directed. (Fig. 4.) (Fig. 5.)

To Make Braid Hats Without a Frame

There are two methods of "free" sewing braid hats, both employed only by the best milliners, as they take too long for low-priced hats. The designer can by these means form the braid into all kinds of odd and artistic shapes, which are afterwards "braced" to hold their form, but the beginner had best take a frame to guide her.

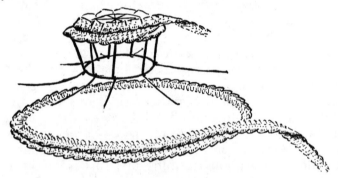

FIG. 6—SHOWING FRAME WITH EDGE WIRE DETACHED, BRIM BEGUN; ALSO CROWN FROM EDGE INWARD

Cut an edge and head wire of the size required, lap and tie firmly; sew the first row of braid on the edge wire as before directed; continue just as on the frame, only you *guide* the shape by the frame, instead of sewing onto it. (See Fig. 6.) When you reach the turned-up row of the headline, sew the wire in a little above the turn inside. If it is a flat crown, the outer ring of wire is cut and sewn onto the flat crown top, or if a dome crown, the ring of the widest circumference; the crown top may be made by either of the foregoing methods. It is easiest now to cut the braces, by measuring the cross wires of the shape you use as model, 4 to 8, according to the softness or stiffness of the braid; allow an inch over for turning over at the edge wire. Pass all the braces under the crown wire in their proper places, back to front, side to side, and half way between these two for the cross braces, and secure firmly in the middle where they all cross. Turn the wires down sharply over edge wire of crown, if the top is flat, or curve them if it is a dome crown; measure off the depth of crown, and bend the wires sharply out at the headline. (See Fig. 5.) Now pass the points of the wires at the back of the head-wire, and out through the braid so they come out about

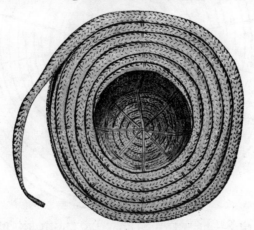

FIG. 7—FREE SEWN BRAID HAT, SHOWING
BRACES DARNED IN BRIM, AND EXTRA ROW
SLIP-STITCHED OVER EDGE WIRE

one-fourth of an inch from the headline on the under brim; *darn* the wire in a straight line out toward the edge wire of brim, taking up the *inner edges* of braid only, by which method the wires will not show at all on the upper side, and very little on the under brim. Pass the wire under the edge wire and turn over in a neat firm clip with the pliers. It is best to mark the places where the wires must come with contrasting bead-headed pins, as the shape of the hat depends on the braces being in correct, even lines from head to edge. (Fig. 7.)

The sides of crown are now finished as before directed. This is an easier way than to make the entire hat and

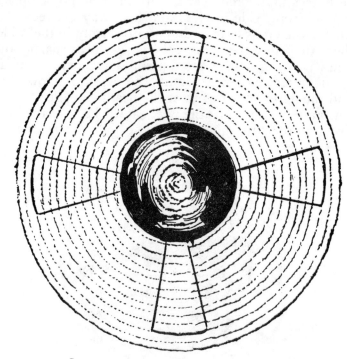

FIG. 8—BRACING STRAW OR LEGHORN BRIM

brace afterward, though this has often to be done. Sometimes the cross braces are not put in at all, but wire loops are buttonhole sewn flat on the brim from the headline out, just to give the necessary support, or enable the designer to obtain and *retain* certain curves, yet retaining the soft effect of an unwired brim. Large unwired crowns are dented into most artistic arrangements, a bandeau or small loop braces alone giving firmness to the headsize. (See Fig. 8.)

Another and often employed way of making "free" sewn hats is to take a frame, loosen the edge wire and middle rings, leaving the crown attached to the cross wires only, sew the brim as before directed, then sew the crown, darn in the braces and attach again to the edge wire. (See Fig. 6.)

Such hats need no underfacing, being neat on both sides, but another row is put under the edge to cover the wire, or this may be some decorative trimming. (See Fig. 7.)

FIG. 9—BRAID GATHERED ON WIRE AT INNER EDGE, DRAWN UP READY TO FORM INTO BRIM

Another and favorite way with the best Parisian designers is to run fine wire through the inner edge of the braid, or if this is not practical it is *darned* in finely; by this wire the rows are drawn to shape and size, the scallops of each row pinned over the inner edge of the previous row till the desired shape is obtained. This then is sewn, usually with the slanted slip or invisible stitch between the two braids, so that the work is absolutely neat on both sides. Such hats can be bent to any shape, and are only braced in some necessary place to hold a particular curve. (See Fig. 9.)

This method of wiring braid is applicable to other uses than the forming of hats, toques or bonnets; in this way one makes rosettes, wings, ruffles, and many a little device that will readily occur to all milliners.

Pointers

Never use more braid than is absolutely necessary; only lap the rows just enough to sew firmly and stretch enough to take out all possible fullness from the inner edges.

Use matching silk for glossy braids, and thread for dull braids. Use matching silk wires for free sewn hats, and matching frames if possible. If you cannot get wire and thread to match, tint them to the required shade with water colors; it is easily and quickly done.

Begin and end all needlefuls with a "tie-stitch," or it will slip through and make gaps in the work. Keep the ends of braid tied round, or they will ravel. (See Fig. 3.) Sew from right to left—unless left-handed.

In order to get the curves in some shapes it is necessary to stretch the *inner* edge and crowd together the scallops; a little experience will show when this is necessary. Remember that your materials are *your servants,* and you may use any expedient that suggests itself, even if not "in the book," so long as you get the right results. Your own judgment must be your guide as to the number of "braces" or "rings" or the size of the wire to use; it depends very much on the braid, the design, and often on the customer.

Toques and Bonnets

Toques are as often sewn free as on a frame, the free sewn form being lightly braced and draped and attached to a bandeau; or they are draped on a small frame that fits the head.

Bonnets are best sewn over frames or molded to

form from previously wired braid, then set on a fitting bandeau or close fitting frame.

Plateau or Plaques

These are a favorite form in which to sew soft pliable braids, the flat mats being made in two ways. One is to make a ring of wire the size the plaque is to be when finished; sew the edge row to this and work inward as directed for the free sewn brim, finishing in the middle as directed for crown, then cutting away the edge wire, if desired soft. Care must be taken that the work is kept perfectly flat and even; and if, when the wire is removed, the work shrinks, which it is very apt to do, because of the stretching of the braid in sewing, one or two rows can be added round the edge.

The other method is to sew from the center out, as directed for the free sewn crown (see Fig. 5). This requires great care to keep the work flat; not to get it full, nor contracted.

Sometimes the mat is required to be oval, or extended more on one side than the other; this effect is obtained by inserting half or quarter rows like gussets or wedges between the rows; extra part rows must never be added on the edge of either plateau or hat; cut a pattern and work by it.

For a double brim plateau, make the under brim like the first, but stop sewing at the headline; wire one of the mats, according to the design required, and slip-stitch the two edges together; bend the braces up, or down, and sew to the bandeau, which is the usual support of plateau hats. (See Bandeaux.)

Hoods

These are another form of sewing up soft braids, especially crins and other braids that drape well. The shape of these hoods is like big jelly bags; they may vary in size, according to the style of hat, toque or bonnet required; they are wide at the edge, running to a round point; a medium size is thirty-six inches around the edge and eighteen inches deep. They are best sewn from the center out, stretching the braid only just enough to get the very gradual increase in circumference. They are also used for draped hat crowns.

"Laced" Braids

This is the method employed to join braids that are of the insertion kind, and do not lap nicely; the lacing is really flat slipstitching, weaving the needle back and forth into the edges of the two braids held in correct position (*i. e.,* drawn to shape) together. This should be done with frame or pattern as guide.

Horsehair Braids

These are the most difficult to sew; very fine thread or silk must be used, and the stitches must be not more than a quarter of an inch long, and on the right side be a back stitch over *one hair only*. A fine running stitch is employed when both sides are to be neat.

Fine leghorn, tuscan, milan and Dunstable braids require the same careful work.

Wings and quills of braid have the outline shaped in wire, and the braid sewn to this in various ways; the edges neatened with braids or bound with materials.

Pressing Straw Shapes

The beauty of hand sewn hats is their soft appearance; hence they are seldom pressed, but if this seems necessary, the brims are laid right side down on a thick ironing cloth, a damp cloth is spread over, and a good, warm iron (not scorching hot) is pressed over; do not push the iron about, but *press,* then move to another spot, letting the iron lap the first a little; when all is done, remove the cloth and go over it with iron only to dry off.

Shapes that cannot be laid flat can be done by two persons by putting the cloth over the upper side of iron and passing the curves *over* this. Always try first without dampening the cloth, as this tends to stiffen the braid, and also there is danger of yellowing white or cream braids.

Small round irons come on purpose for the insides of crowns, and are to be used with a circular movement.

Bracing

Leghorn flats, unless for children, are seldom left in their original shape, *i. e.,* a flat, round, even brim; to enable the milliner to curve and bend them, they are "braced" with wire. This should be a finer number than that used in frames, and of course matching the hat in color, as must also the sewing silk or thread.

Some leghorns, chips and felts are so soft and firm that the stitches—a fine buttonhole stitch, ½ an inch long—can be taken on the same side as the brace, picking up a fraction under the wire, and laying the *buttonhole stitch* alongside the wire, not on it.

But it may be found necessary to take the stitches through, in which case it must be crossed over one fiber only in a chip or Leghorn, and in a felt the needle is passed back into the *same place where it came out,* but at a slant, so that the stitch is really taken in the thickness of the felt.

The number and size of the braces, and if to be over or under the brim, depend entirely on the shape to be developed, and where the trimming will best hide the braces, though as these are absolutely necessary, and of fine matching wire and neat work, one does not object to their being seen.

But if a hat is to be curved up, naturally the wire would be put on the upper brim, and *vice versa*.

Having decided on the length and width of the loops, the wire is cut off, allowing an inch at each end extra to run up inside or outside of the crown; these two ends are sewn first, the outside corners pinned in place, then the surface wire sewn as directed. (See Fig. 8.)

In the bracing of lace hats the wires usually run quite to the edge, but good taste and judgment will always direct to the correct proceeding in special work.

LESSON VII

CHILDREN'S MILLINERY

CHILDREN'S millinery, like mourning, is considered so much a special branch, that few milliners comparatively care to, or can, handle it satisfactorily; yet as no one knows when they may be called upon to execute a special order, it is essential that they know how to do it.

In general millinery, although no stitches may be visible, as a rule, little fine work is necessary; in children's work it is just the opposite, all must be done in fine sewing, much of which is visible and forms in fact the key to the design. A good children's milliner seldom is as good at other classes of work, except shirred hats, or "lingerie" effects, just that smaller class that require fine visible work, while a good general milliner will make her children's designs too old, or depending more on the trimming for effect than on the work.

Taking the Measures

Of course fashions change for children as for adults, but not to the same extent; it is at most a change in detail, rather than in construction. A child's hat or bonnet must fit well on the head, and if measures cannot be taken from real heads (for these vary very much indeed) use a wax head, and see to it that the head sizes are deep and wide enough to fit well. By studying the six diagrams, a correct idea of the methods of measurement will be obtained. Take diagram 1. Pin a tape around the face a to b; another from c to c around back. Measure back over the head from a to middle of line c-c; call this point d; measure from the tape a-b in front of the ears round back of head e to c, note the measure from c to c, round back of head, and from c to c around the face, which cuts out several inches under the chin.

96

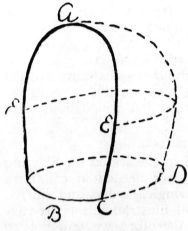

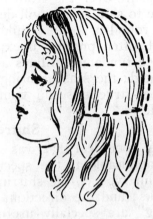

DIAGRAM I—MEASURING
FOR A CLOSE BONNET

DIAGRAM 2—MEASURING
FOR CROWN OF BONNET
WITH BRIM

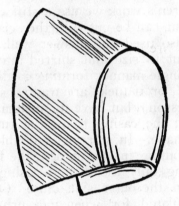

DIAGRAM 3—MEASURING
FOR A HAT

DIAGRAM 4—FOUNDATION
FOR BONNET

In diagram 2—for a Granny bonnet the measurements are almost the same, but the line a to b is taken about 1½ inches up on the head above the forehead and the line c to c comes also a little farther back. For a hat, diagram 3, the circular measure is around the fullest part of the head just above the brow, and from this measure over the head from front to back, and from side to side, which will determine if the headsize should be round or oval. Children's heads are undeveloped, and often present unexpected formations. On these three fundamental lines all children's chapeaux are designed; the seasons bringing their modifications in the super-structures and trimmings; but foundations vary little.

Shirred Effects

A good deal that was said in the lesson on Shirring is applicable to the special work needed in children's millinery, i. e., the shirring, single, double, and shirred tucks; and the directions and illustration for "fly-running" are specially useful; therefore we will not go over this ground again, but note the *differences* in the methods for the two classes of work.

Instead of wire or wire frames being used for children's work we use a stiff cord; it is pliable, will bend, but can be cut with the scissors; featherbone reeds are also used and answer well. These reeds or cords are cut to size and shirred into the material in either the single manner forming cordings, as in Fig. 11 of Lesson V, or if tucks are wanted shir like Figs. 3 or 4 (same lesson), but have the material double, and run the reeds in the casing below the tucks, thereby drawing it to shape. In shirring a double brim with tucks, the side coming inside, or next the face, should be plain, showing only the shirred casings, the tucks being laid up on the outer side only. Of course this must be calculated for when measuring for the brim. For instance: if the brim is 5 inches deep, with three two-inch tucks at the edge, and three ½-inch tucks lower down, you must cut your strip 28 inches wide, which allows 5 inches inside and out, 1 inch each side for turn-up against crown, 1 inch take-up or making, 3 inches for the three ½-inch tucks, and 12 inches for the three 2-inch edge tucks; this to be folded so that the *middle* edge tuck comes on the edge of brim with a wire casing below, and the other deep tucks close against this, joined by another casing. This means that you fold your piece with 12½ inches for the inside, and the rest for the outside.

In shirring for either cordings or casings it may be run first and the reeds put in after, then drawn to shape, the threads drawn up and fastened off; the reeds are either cut, lapped and securely twisted together with thread, or where there is no back brim the ends are sewn to the material and bound over so they cannot work out and scratch the child. Or the reeds are cut to size of graduated rings, lapped and secured and the material shirred directly over them; this method is best for hats and bonnets that have a back brim, as directed in Lesson V.

To get a good fitting head it is not enough to take the measures and construct the head piece from these, as the same measures may apply to variously shaped heads; one must take notice of any oddity in the head formation as bulges or slants can be allowed for in plaiting up the crown foundation.

Cut your muslin for foundation, a square of your *largest* measure, cut a strip on the straight 2 inches wide, and in length the combined measures of face and back of neck, with 2 inches over for turning corners and joining. Fold this, the two edges to middle, lay in a strip of ribbon wire, fold over and baste, letting the join—1-inch lap—come at the back; turn up two corners indicating the points c to c in Diagram 1. Thus you have the outline of your head. Pin the muslin square to the top (a in Diagram 1) and to the middle back according to the measure given; pin the middle sides also to the band according to measure taken from e to e. Then putting one hand inside the crown it is shaped and the plaits laid. If the child's head is large around from e to e, the deepest plaits are laid at and on either side of this line; if it is large at top it must be allowed for in the plaits there, but in any case the

plaits on both sides must correspond, and run out evenly and flat from the band towards the head. After pinning up the shape, trim off the projecting corners, and
baste round. On such a foundation various kinds of
crowns are built, and the band makes a firm support for
any kind of a brim. This crown is also the foundation
for the "Dutch" cap or bonnet, which is always more or
less in vogue in some form.

Fancy Hats and Bonnets

Sometimes the brims may be shirred in straight
lines, when the reeds are put in after, but frequently
the casings must be graduated from wider in front and
at sides to narrow spacings at the back, where the
brim narrows; this is easily marked by measuring and
creasing the material, though when using soft silks
or velvet the lines are best basted. Hats either of
pliable straw, Leghorn, horsehair or felt, with good
deep crowns and wide brims, are easily and successfully converted into handsome children's bonnets; the
backs either shortened or entirely cut away for about
4 inches against the nape of the neck, and the brim
then curved or folded so that it gradually increases in
depth towards the sides and top. A band of ribbon
wire sewn around the inside of the crown is sufficient
support; but if the brim is too floppy, a few braces of
fine wire can be button-hole sewn in, the ends of the
pear-shaped loops running up inside the crown, and
covered by the folded muslin headband enclosing the
ribbon wire. The necessity of securing and covering
all wires so they cannot possibly work out cannot be
too strongly insisted on.

Putting On Ties

Then the ties are often another source of worry to
a child; they are intended to hold the hat or bonnet *on*,
yet frequently they are so placed that when tied under
the chin they pull the bonnet *off!* When the brim
slants much back at the ears it will be found necessary

100

to put an elastic from about 2½ inches up on each side to go under the chin, or *narrow* soft tie ribbons, then the ties that come from the ears of the bonnet can be tied loosely in a decorative bow, otherwise they must be tried in various poses, till a comfortable and efficient place is found to sew on the tie ribbons.

Everything about children's wear should be soft, no harsh materials, no hard ridges; they should be so comfortable as to be unconscious of their clothing.

FIG. I—"DUTCH" BONNET. FIG. 2—"DUTCH" BONNET.
SIDE AND BACK   FRONT VIEW

The "Dutch" Bonnet

An illustration is given of a pretty "Dutch" bonnet which can be carried out in straw and chiffon, with

101

trimming of lace, ribbon and flowers, or in crêpe de chine like the model; silk or velvet, substituting two or three little ostrich tips or silk pompons for the flowers. This style of bonnet can be made up in a great many ways; the kerchief back can be changed to a smooth or ruffled effect. (See Figs. 1 and 2.)

To such a bonnet the lining must be carefully fitted. Cut a horseshoe shaped piece to fit flat on the back; cut a strip to fit around the face, and meet the crown piece, gather one edge of the strip and run on the crown piece, evening the fullness so that it fits nicely in, turn in the other edge, pin into the bonnet *when*

FIG. 3—"DUTCH" BONNET WITH CORONET

completed, and slipstitch it edge to edge, also around the back, so that the inside presents a perfectly neat appearance.

Fig. 3 is the "Dutch" bonnet in another form, hav-

102

ing a coronet front turned right up from the face. The frame of this is of cape net, cut just like a large hat crown with a piece scooped out for the back. This was sewn over with fine straw braid, the coronet was "free" sewn, that is sewn and shaped without any foundation. Afterwards two rows of reeds were darned, or threaded round *in the braid,* and narrow Mechlin lace sewn round in slightly full ruffles, covering the face of the coronet. A twist of ribbon, similar to those outside went around the face line. This model would be very good in shirred material, either on a net frame, or the shape formed by reeds. In this also the lining is fitted and slipstitched in.

FIG. 5—"DUTCH" BONNET WITH WINGS. BACK VIEW

Another variation of the "Dutch" bonnet is shown in Fig. 5, the close-fitting cap, which is of fine white silk muslin shirred on cords, leaving full puffs be-

tween; the crown is in the shape of a closed magnet
rather than a horseshoe. The last puff runs under to
the nape of the neck, and to the face line. Here are
set on a pair of wings, as shown in the back view; these
are of the muslin, plain on the back, done in cordings
on the front, edged with double ruffle of narrow Val
lace. The foundation of these wings is of muslin with
wire sewn in the edge, the ends being sewn firmly on
the *outside* of the cap, a double ruffle of the lace going
on after, which neatens the join. A full puff of the
muslin goes around the face, the trimming being of soft
ribbon and baby roses. As will be seen, the wings are
curved backward, and may be adjusted at will; this cap
is more suitable for baby boys.

FIG. 6—"EMPIRE" BONNET. BACK VIEW

Fig. 6, an Empire bonnet, is a large flat-brimmed hat
with wide bell crown; the brim is cut away from half
the crown and folded forward, making a double-brim
effect, the brimless portion of the crown forming the
back. The brim is drawn in and curved in flutes low
down on the right, but the flutes spring higher on the
left, a full rosette and cluster of flowers being set below,

a rosette only finishing the right side; the ties cross the
base of crown at the back. Around the face line in
front was a double hand-plaited ruche of white mousseline, a rosette and a few flowers tucked under the brim
on the left, and small rosettes centered with the little
blossoms below each ear; it is a most attractive model,
and would reproduce well in felt or beaver; or can be
made in velvet and silk over a fine cape net foundation.

FIG. 7—CHILD'S 1830 BONNET. FACE VIEW

A beautiful design in children's bonnets is shown in
Fig. 7, which gives the back and front views of this
Parisian model, adapted from the modes of 1830, and
named the "Bébé." The foundation is a net crown like
an ordinary hat crown, of 20 inches circumference and
a depth of 3 inches; this is of cape net, stiffened with
tape wire and bound with white silk; the top of this
crown is covered with plain muslin. Over this is set a
cape of muslin, shirred on featherbone reeds so that it
flares away from the crown at the base about 2 inches on
each side and 1 inch in front, but is gathered close
around the top of the crown, and ends on each side at
the ears, projecting a little here. Around the edge of

this is a frill of Val lace 2 inches wide, which drops well below the crown. Below this, filling in the space between the crown and cap, is a frill of narrow Val run on each side of a strip of muslin 3 inches wide, which is box plaited through the middle, doubled over and sewn on about 1 inch above the silk binding, but *not* crossing the back.

Above this we find a strip of muslin 4 inches wide, edged with the 2-inch Val; this is deeply box plaited and sewn round upper edge of crown 1 inch from top, gradually narrowing to the ears on each side of the back.

Now comes the superstructure. The shell-like brim is a straight strip of muslin shirred single over ten reeds, the first 32 inches long, the last fitting around the front of the crown above the box-plaited frill, the other reeds curving in and sewn on the crown, as is clearly shown in the picture. These reeds, be they featherbone or shirring cords, are pliable and soft, and can be easily bent under and neatly and firmly sewn. The edge cord is covered by a border of English embroidery, in four wide scallops, which is set on with a fine *soft* cording. The crown, which is also a straight strip shirred on 10 cords, is set on before the brim, the two scallops of embroidery around the crown top covering the joins.

Around the crown under the embroidery goes a "wreath" trimming made of No. 3 blue satin ribbon; this is made of short loops sewn on a ½-inch strip of muslin, three little loops in a row, similar to Fig. 15 in Lesson X. Tucked in between the two ruffles of lace on each side are rosettes of the ribbon, centered with buttons made of the tie ribbon doubled and gathered through the middle, and the edges caught in shells. As will be seen, the ties are sewn to the *cap,* where it is brought out square on each side. It will take 9 yards of the wide Val, 4 of the fine, 10 yards narrow ribbon and 2½ of the tie ribbon.

This would be a charming model done in silk, silk embroidery, and chiffon ruffles, and is given here to show the elaborate construction often found in Parisian designs of children's millinery.

Baby's Cap or Bonnet

In Fig. 9 we give a pretty design for a baby's shirred bonnet or cap, which is, however, capable of many variations; it may be of washable lawn or net, or of silk muslin, or of some thin silk. The trimming may be of lace or fine embroidered lawn; the bows and ties of fine hemmed lawn or silk, or of ribbon. If of silk, the lining is of silk; if of lawn, the lining is also of lawn; in either case cut like foundation (Diagram 5 and 6) to fit perfectly inside the completed cap.

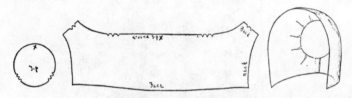

DIAGRAM 5   DIAGRAM 6

FLAT FOUNDATION AND SAME MADE UP FOR INFANT'S CAP; ALSO LINING

The foundation is cut from fine crinoline muslin, in shape like Diagram 5, in size according to the measurements taken (see Diagram 1); this is put together as shown in Diagram 6; the front only turned over a strip of tape wire, the two ends being turned up flat and enclosed in a bit of lawn so they cannot work out; the back is turned up over a bit of cord or tape to hold the shape.

The piece of material for the shirred cap is a strip cut from two to three times the length of the face measure, according to the texture of the material; of thin silk double or less, of lawn the same, but of chiffon or mousseline de soie three times is required.

107

The width, as shown, will take half as much again as the width of foundation, measuring from middle of tip to edge of face line; this allows for the cordings and turn-over at the face line, a tiny turning at center of tip and a *little* puffiness between the cordings.

FIG. 9—INFANT'S SHIRRED MOUSSELINE CAP

This shirring is done direct on the cords, as directed in Figs. 5 and 11 of Lesson V. The three complete rings on the tip are formed and laid down ready for

103

use inside each other, the other cords are then cut,—all by measuring around the foundation; the spaces may vary, of course, according to fancy, or the amount of work one wishes to put in. The cords are laid down in their order so no mistake is made in picking them up for the shirring. Now measure off from tip edge of material to first ring and lay this in place, creasing (or basting) the line to be shirred. (N. B.—The *back* of the material should be *closed* in a slant before beginning the shirring.) Turn the marked line over the ring and shir the material in a casing over it, drawing up the gathers as the work proceeds. Lay second and third rings in and shir in in the same way; next, take the straight cords in succession, sewing the ends firmly till the face is reached. Now gather the tip edge on the wrong side, draw up quite tight, secure the ravelled edge so it cannot work out, turn, flatten out, and sew invisibly to center of tip. Secure first and third rings by tiny stitches among the gathers, and stitches about an inch long inside foundation.

To ensure the fullness being even it is best to mark with contrasting thread the middle and quarters at face and tip line, the lines of fulling should run in even lines from tip to face. The ends of the cords are now firmly sewn in place on foundation, the ravelled edge next face gathered and sewn down, also the first cord next face line; the others need no sewing. Fasten off all threads and bind all around with a double fold of the material.

The lace is gathered and sewn on inside, several full plaits being placed across top, the lace is turned over to the outside, caught by "tie-stitches" in pretty flutes, the extra fullness at top being arranged in a few puffs that come *forward;* the simple bow setting against them. Tie a three-yard length of ribbon in a simple little bow in the middle, sew this on back of bonnet, carry ribbon along the back to ears, form a little bow on each and let three-quarters of a yard fall as ties on each side; sew all firmly. Now set in the ready prepared lining, made just as the foundation; turn the seams *inside* and slipstitch edge to edge. If an extra ruche of narrow lace or plaited chiffon is desired inside against the face it is put in before the head lining.

FIG. 10—LITTLE GIRL'S DRESSY BONNET. SIDE VIEW

Figs. 10 and 11 show a lovely bonnet for a girl from 4 to 7 years old. It can be carried out in many ways. The foundation is of fine cape net, a crown like a plain flat hat crown that fits the head as shown in

Diag. 3, with a plain brim of the net, shaped as shown in Fig. 13, Lesson I (Frames), and curved gradually to one inch at the back from three inches in front and at sides.

Cut round tip about seven inches in diameter, cut side crown to fit this, a straight strip three inches wide;

FIG. 11—LITTLE GIRL'S DRESSY BONNET.   BACK VIEW

set rings of wire on tip one-half inch from edge; close side crown; wire round both edges; snip margin of tip, and through this margin down over side crown and sew down. Cut brim with a three-quarter inch margin

111

BACK AND FRONT VIEW OF TWO PRETTY BONNETS

at inner edge, snip and turn this up against crown
and sew firmly, allow a one-half inch margin at edge,
turn this over a fine firm wire and sew flat under
wire; be sure to lap all wires well and secure firmly.

Now cover crown and brim *plainly* with the material
the bonnet is to be made of; next puff a strip rather
full over brim, gathering it into the headsize inside,
and around base of crown outside, gather a round
piece rather larger than entire crown, set over crown
and draw up around headline; arrange two strips of
lace or embroidery across crown flat, as shown, gather
frill of same and set around headline.

The shaped brim is bent up in a deep curve in the
middle front and some shallow waves at sides, but

112

the strip gathered full over brim should be deeper than foundation, thus giving a fluffy soft effect, entirely hiding even the outline of foundation brim.

The trimming is shown as of ribbon only, but may be varied by small flowers or ostrich tips.

This bonnet can be carried out for winter wear; in either case it needs an elastic band from near the top under the chin, so that the strings may be loosely tied.

FRONT AND BACK VIEW OF TWO PRETTY BONNETS

LESSON VIII

MOURNING MILLINERY

MOURNING is a distinct and very important branch of millinery, and many clever designers command excellent salaries, devoting their entire artistic abilities to this work alone. The scope of materials is limited, the colors restricted to black, white, and various shades of the blue lavenders and violets; and occasionally greys; in England, cardinal is added to this list, accepted because of its ecclesiastical use. Therefore a designer has a more difficult task to evolve from the small varieties at her disposal, headgear at once suitable, becoming and artistic.

Materials

The materials used are, first of all crape, in black and white. This comes in a number of grades of quality, some dull, some glossy, some crisp, some so soft, that if gathered into a handful it will not crush; but of all makes the "waterproof" is to be preferred. Next comes crêpe de chine in black and white, the lusterless kind; chiffon, mousseline de soie, crêpe-lisse, grenadine and tulle. In silks the rich dull grosgrain, peau de soie, and Ottomans of rich, heavy cord; and uncut velvet, in England known as "Terry" velvet; this comes in several sizes of welt, from very fine to quite a heavy cord; it may be used for deep mourning, having a dull, deep surface not unlike crape; it is admirable to cover frames, just as one would use velvet, and accentuate the depth of the mourning by crape trimmings. It is handsome also used to bind and trim hats of crêpe de chine, dull felt, chip, Neapolitan, etc., as one would use velvet in colored work. Brussels nets and nun's veilings also come into use for veils, etc.

Wings, quills (Paradise and aigrette if permitted or desired), dull black jet, bright jet and *white* jet, all find

114

their appropriate place and time in the various grades of mourning which will be considered later. We must know how to cut, make and combine to get the best possible effects and most pleasing results from the few materials at our disposal.

FIG. I—CRAPE. ON STRAIGHT. NATURAL
GRAIN IS DIAGONAL

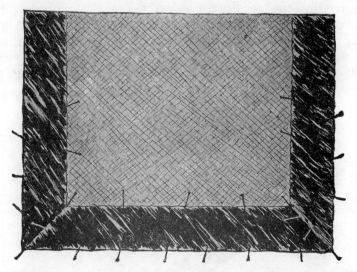

FIG. 3—NET VEIL, APPLIED HEM, SHOWING MITRE
JOIN AND THE TWO STRAIGHT DIAGONALS
MEETING AT JOINS

115

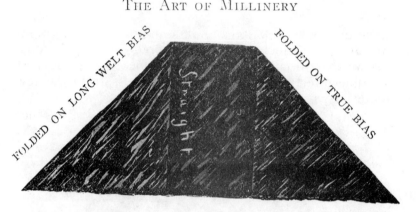

FIG. 2—SHOWING CRAPE FOLDED ON THE
TRUE AND LONG BIAS

The Uses of Crape

Crape has four distinct "grains"; in the natural grain (Fig. 1) the welts run obliquely from selvedge to selvedge, the widths of various makes vary, but the average of good crape is 42 inches, which gives a bias of about 53 inches. Now this bias is of two kinds; folding the crape over on the *true bias* we get the welts in straight lines *across* the bias (Fig. 2); folding the

FIG. 4—LATTICED CROWN, SHOW-
ING CROSS AND LONG BIAS

piece over in the opposite direction, also on a true bias, we get the welts in long parallel lines; while if we wish to use the crape *along* the selvedge, instead of across, we get again the diagonal welt, but in the opposite slant as from selvedge to selvedge, which fact enables you to mitre corners of hems applied on net or gauze veils so that the welts radiate *from* the joins (Fig. 3). The designer naturally takes advantage of these several aspects of the material to combine them in effective ways, thus overcoming her limitations very charmingly, especially by the combination of the two bias welts.

Folds cut in the two ways joined by the "lacing" stitch with fine crape thread and braided or latticed together to form crowns or brims are very effective. (Fig. 4.) Such crowns may be large or small, the folds may vary from one-third of an inch to one and one-half inches wide, but are best made on a foundation; beginning at the center cross, and working to each side; pin each fold at the edge of the foundation, till all are laid, then baste round, and catch underneath so they will keep their place. This lattice work can be done direct on the frame, then if closely laid, it should need no sewing except around the edge; it can also be used for turban brims.

Braided folds for brims may be on the long or cross bias, and on the straight if all the welts run the same way. (Fig. 5.)

FIG. 5—SECTION OF BRAIDED BRIM ON LONG BIAS

Crape done on cords looks best on the true bias, or on the straight, which also holds true of shirrings, tucks, plaitings, ruches; the long welt bias allowing the work to spread, and spoiling the harmony of lines. All this class of work is more troublesome in crape than almost any other material, hence needs extra care in cutting, pinning, basting; which with accurate measurements and good work will ensure satisfactory results.

*FIG. 6—JOINING CRAPE CUT ON STRAIGHT
BIAS

In measuring for tucks, etc., the same methods as for ordinary millinery are employed, but from the nature of the material it follows that less fullness will give better effects, but this again depends on the quality of the crape and should be tested. All joins must be *along* the welt, never across. (Figs. 6 and 7.)

For draperies, bows, folds, the crape may be either on the straight or the cross lines, according to how the hat is made; these two lines should, however, never be mixed.

Slipstitched, or "French" folds are very effective in crape. They are made in the same way as velvet, extra care being required not to catch the under side of the fold, or it will "twist" badly. To make folds roll— a pretty and effective method for crape work—a narrower strip of interlining muslin or black crêpe francaise is laid inside; or one makes also "corded" folds, by running into single cut folds "crape cord," which

118

comes in various thicknesses; another way is to cut strips of black sheet wadding, roll them to roundness

BIAS
FIG. 7—JOINING CRAPE CUT ON BIAS

between the flat hands and lay this roll inside folds, with an inner covering of thin interlining muslin. A succession of such folds around the upturned brim of toque or turban is very rich.

When puffing crape the plaits must be laid deeper than in velvet, as the springy nature of the material causes it to disarrange itself, and the puffs and folds need neat "tying" to keep them in place. Draping is for the same reason more difficult than in velvet, but a little practice with old crape (or cotton crape cloth at 15 or 20 cents the yard) will soon enable the earnest worker to handle her crape with assurance of perfect results. (Silk muslin at 20 cents is a good substitute for the gauze materials and net to practice on.)

To make folded bands for knots or twisted trimmings, allow plenty in width, so that when the folds are laid and *basted* along the middle of the piece the two edges may be turned under and "cat-stitched" down on the trimming; if the strip does not allow of this, it should be narrowly "roll hemmed" and mounted on a strip of thin crape. Short pieces of laid folds can be held in place with pins till sewn in place. Folds can also be held as laid and pinned, by securing with *cross* lines of stitches on the wrong side at intervals of several inches.

For gathered or plaited rosettes and ruches the crape may be on the straight, or cross bias, the strip, if thin

119

crape, may be double, but if heavy crape, use single and make a nice roll hem along the edge. An applied hem is also very useful; this is run on one side, turned over and slipstitched down edge to edge, so it forms a distinct roll. Such a hem on net bias, for instance, should be quite deep and round, cut 2½ inches at least through the bias.

When desiring the front of toque or bonnet to be folds, and the other side plain, cover the frame (wire) with interlining muslin, and first binding the edge, sew on the folds, then *fit in* the reverse side and slipstitch the edge to the bind. The same method is employed in underfacing a large flat hat with folds, the upper covering being slipped on after the folds are on and slipstitched to the edge, or if for some reason this is not practical, great care must be exercised not to catch the upper covering when running on the folds; another way is to cut a correct pattern in thin crape or muslin, run the folds on this, and then slipstitch this on edge to edge.

The ideas possible of use in mourning millinery are just as varied as in the colored work, this supplying the best models for real up-to-date mourning, suitable materials from the mourning list being substituted. For instance, crape, uncut velvet, or rich thick silk may take the place of velvet, other materials and trimmings being selected with care, so that the *value of harmonies* may be retained.

As we do not generally use ostrich feathers in mourning here, a handsome arrangement of ribbons, wings, or ruches will often replace these on a model, and dull jet will take the place of brilliant ornaments.

White crape is now used quite a good deal even for all-crape hats as an under facing, or in bands and folds; and all white crape, made up just as the black would be, is considered equally deep.

The lighter materials all find use in the various grades of mourning. In using corded silks, all the grain, be it bias or straight, must run the same way on the chapeau, and ribbons must match. Crêpe de chine and chiffon are used in combination with both crape and silk; and mousseline de soie and crêpe-lisse are used for tucked and shirred underbrims, also in summer chapeaux in folds and shirrings for entire hats.

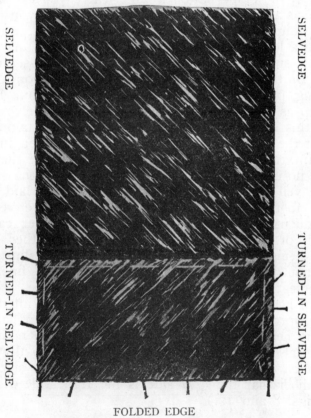

FOLDED EDGE

FIG. 8—PREPARING HEM OF CRAPE VEIL

Brussels net is used mostly for veils, but plain covered (wire) frames, with fine crape folds slipstitched on the net in several circles, make becoming hats. Dull white silk on white silk Brussels net is also correct, and very handsome.

121

In using flowers, either white or black, no speck of yellow or green must be visible; violets can be purchased with white or purple stems, made purposely for mourning.

To Hem a Crape Veil

Lay the crape flat on a table where you can use one side as a guide to pin the selvedge to, then you can get a straight line at the end of the table for your hem. Use a long yard stick and blue pencil; the marks will show sufficiently to trim off the unevenness, and the set of the hem, wide or narrow, depends on the end being perfectly straight. Now fold up your hem as deep as you want it, two, four, even to twelve inches, do this by accurate measurement, and *pin,* taking care that the selvedges are level. Now go over the hem again, turning in the edge, pin closely, see that there are no uneven places, and baste along. If the sides of the veil are to be hemmed, these are best laid before the foot hem; but even in quite expensive veils one frequently sees the selvedges left; in either case the ends of the deep hem are slipstitched together. After the hems have been carefully prepared the slipstitching is not difficult, use fine crape thread and fine, short needles; *no stitches* may show on *either* side.

In hemming the two ends of a long veil intended to be worn first over the face, then thrown back, the front hem should be a third less in width than the back one, also, it is done on the reverse side, so that when *thrown back,* the two will be on the same side. Remember that the *hem* side is the right side of a veil. (Figs. 8 and 12.)

Applied Hems

These are used on veils of Brussels net, which should be treated just as the crape to get it perfectly straight, and the hem—cut on the straight—must be cut with equal care. The net is wider usually than the crape, and may be cut away, but allow for a hem of from one to two inches down each side, unless a hem of crape is carried down as shown in Fig. 3, in which case the joins must be perfectly fitted at the corners, "mitred" together, pinned and slipstitched. It may be thought that the hem would go all right if it is run edge to edge, turned up, and slipstitched down, but it will not; it must be carefully pinned, basted and slipstitched along *both* edges; only so can the corners be made to look perfectly neat and workmanlike. Applied folds above a hem must be cut by the rule, the edges turned under, pinned and basted in place before slipstitching. When the hem down the sides is much narrower than the foot hem, it is not mitred, but run just under the edge of the foot hem, this being slipstitched across it.

Sometimes one is required to make the hems double; then they are prepared by running a basting thread along the *fold*, so as to keep them perfectly flat and true, and the net is set in *between* the two turned-in edges, closely pinned, carefully basted, and then the two edges slipstitched together; for this a rather heavier silk thread is best, as these veils are quite heavy, and a very close stitch is needed. By the bye, never darn pins in *along* your crape, etc.; always let the heads be *above* your hems. See illustrations.

To Cover and Prepare Frames

French milliners never use buckram frames for mourning work; indeed, they seldom use them at all. Stiff cape net is best for plain covered hats; if braces are needed, be sure to overlay them with a bias strip of muslin, and carefully fit thin interlining muslin over the frame, so that no gloss or the holes of the net may be perceptible. Thin black cashmere makes an excellent under covering for crape (white for white crape, but silk for crêpe de chine or chiffon), but in cheap work alpaca is a good substitute. Muslin is not good; it gets rusty before the crape, and gives this a bad color. The edges of frames are better bound with a narrow

strip of wadding under the cashmere, and silk hats
should have the fitted layer of wadding the same as in
colored work.

Wire frames must be first covered with muslin, then
with cheap crape, on which the drapings, etc., are done,
but thick folds and shirrings may be put right on the
muslin or cashmere. In fitting plain facings, take care

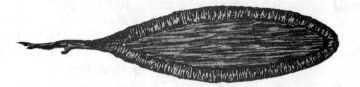

FIG. 10—CRAPE QUILL LONG BIAS, BOUND CROSS BIAS

FIG. 9
MAKING CRAPE WING

FIG. 11—CRAPE PETAL,
FORMED ON WIRE

you do not stretch the crape out of line; it looks very
bad to see the welts pulled awry; they should cross the
middle front diagonally, unless you have the entire brim
on the bias; then the welts run straight from the edge
in from front to back, but this is not as pretty.

Shirred effects are measured, prepared and put in the
same as velvet or silk. Clusters of tucks, folds or cord-

ings either in silk or crape or the two combined are always effective.

To make wings or quills, bend the desired shape in wire, pin this on a piece of crape, turn a narrow margin over the wire and run it in. Bind with a roll hem of crape or silk; fine jet may be used for wings or quills of net; a big pompon of slender willow leaves made in this way is a handsome trimming. (Figs. 9-10.)

Wild and full roses can be made of scraps of crape, by bending the petal shape in fine lace wire, and stretching over this a bit of crape, tying the ravellings around the twisted wire stem. (Fig. 11.) Black flower stamens may be used as centers, or just a bit of wadding twisted round a double wire stem, with a bit of silk over, and the petals, few or many, arranged around this and firmly twisted on with strong thread. Black flower cusps or a bit of silk cut round with a hole in the middle finishes the flowers underneath. (See Lesson XIII, on Making Silk Flowers.)

Thus the scraps may be turned into beautiful trimmings, and the apprentices kept busy during the dull season.

Correct Mourning

It is true that the making of mourning belongs in the domain of the workroom, but what shall be made is decided in the showroom, and the saleswoman is expected to be always conversant with Fashion's latest dictum, few customers being at the time of bereavement in a condition to give more than the absolutely necessary attention to the details of their sartorial expression of grief. Hence the order often comes in the simplest form —"Send us the correct things for widow, daughters, sisters, &c., &c."—leaving the entire detail to the saleswoman, who is supposed to know her customers, and what will be becoming as well as suitable.

Years ago the "becomingness" was not considered; the ugliest things only were permitted as tokens of woe, a sort of metaphorical "sackcloth and ashes," but about

20 years ago changes began to appear, crape bonnets became more ornate, one began to copy Paris colored hats and toques in mourning materials, and the weight of veils began to be lessened, mainly because physicians pronounced them dangerous to health, four yards and more of heavy crape often being put in one widow's veil.

Of course, the change to better, more sensible modes has been gradual, but Paris and New York have combined in the evolution of mourning, and London is in touch with both.

Widow's Mourning

The English fashion for the widow, young or old, to wear in the house a dainty little "Marie Stuart" coif of white crêpe Lisse, with long white tulle veil floating from the back, is charming and as becoming to the widow of 20 as to her mother, but English mourning retains much of the old-time stiffness, except in the class that comes much in contact with Paris.

The French widow never for one moment loses sight of effect. If she must wear mourning, then that must be made to enhance her good points, and so contrived that it shall add to and not detract from her charms— hence the frequent relief of a facing of white crape in her black crape hat or bonnet, these following the prevailing mode as closely as possible. But it is the veil that receives the greatest attention, as its arrangement makes or mars the entire toilette, and its length must tell her story to the world.

Veils were formerly worn to the hem of the train at the back and to the knees in front; the weight was unbearable except for such women as rarely walked; even then they were very trying. The weight was relieved by an arrangment lifting and draping them slightly on the left hip, and sometimes letting one shoulder support part of the heavy folds, but even then a strong back comb was (and is) necessary to keep the chapeau on the head.

Now the veil for the deepest mourning does not come lower than the knees at the back, and to the waist in front; in fact, it should be so arranged that the prayer book may be held comfortably below the hem, as lifting this will break it.

The rigorous law is that this veil is to be worn three months, but, as a matter of fact, many widows wear the crape veil only six weeks, then throw it back and wear a Brussels net or tulle face veil hemmed with crape; many have the veil cut off and redraped to get rid of the weight, which is perfectly sensible, and in three months more this veil may be changed for one of net with deep crape hem; this also is later shortened, and a narrower hem allowed.

The orthodox rule for a widow is crape for two years, but now one is considered long enough, the second year dull silk, crêpe de chine, chiffon, &c., taking its place.

Pure white crape, made up and used in the same way as black, is equally deep, and now soft dove and steel gray are being worn, even to the long veil.

The "Marie Stuart" bonnet for first widow's mourning is no longer the only correct thing; they are not becoming to all, and the changes in modern coiffure make modifications imperative; therefore, a small toque often replaces the bonnet, with a touch of white near the face, put in *after the funeral*.

The veil, if not too heavy, is quite becoming to most women; hence French women often adopt it for grades of mourning that really do not call for this; the taste, inclination, and *purse* of the mourner being at present the chief law as to the style and duration of mourning. It may, however, be taken for granted that in deep first mourning rich simplicity in design and line of veil is in best taste; later more ornate and picturesque designs may be suggested, but from first to last the chapeaux must be becoming.

A woman of position must have the ultra-correct things in town, but in the country she may substitute a crape-trimmed net or plain chiffon veil on a crape toque or small, plain crape hat.

127

The automobile is responsible for some really charming innovations in mourning veils, and even white shirred chiffon ties are in order, when a white chiffon or crape underfacing or ruche is worn.

FIG. 12—WIDOW'S VEIL OVER FACE

Elderly widows wear longer veils than young ones (though the latter *may* wear them as long as they please), the hem being 12 to 16 inches wide, the front

128

hem one-third narrower. Bombazine or thick grenadine with deep hemstitched hems is also correct for elderly women, but the young widow keeps to crape till she

FIG. 13—VEIL DRAPED ACROSS

may wear the net and crape hem, and for change a silk nun's-veiling veil.

A tall woman will need a veil not less than 90 inches long, and of course the full width of the crape, while about 70 inches will be long enough for a short woman.

Draping Veils

If a customer objects to wearing the heavy crape over her face, and many do, after the funeral, let her send it back, take it off and arrange the narrower front hem in a plaited fan or other arrangement suitable to the bonnet, and pin on gracefully to fall over the back, and send her a "sewing silk" or fine gauze veil with

PARISIAN MOURNING CHAPEAU WITH SMALL VEIL

folds of crape, for the face; such crape veils are cut from 1½ to 2 yards long with 9-inch hem for the back, and five inches at the other end, and both hems made on the same side. The toque or bonnet for such an arrangement need have only the brim made with folds, &c.; the veil covers the crown at first, and later can be made to trim it, drape it, the veil falling behind.

A square veil, made the width of the crape, is effectively put on with the points forming cascades on each side of the back, the veil being folded three parts over, and pinned in deep double folds on each side of the back. If used on a hat, this veil may have one corner carried around the left, partly over the crown, to the front; the opposite point hangs down the middle of the back; the two sides are plaited so the points hang in graceful deep folds over one shoulder and back.

A veil two yards long may be laid *across* a toque or

FIG. 14—SMART CRAPE TURBAN

small hat, in which case it is hemmed all round evenly; the middle of one long side is pinned on the middle back of hat, the sides plaited up so that two points hang down the back, and two at the shoulders, in double inverted box plaits. (See Fig. 13.)

When part of the long veil is to fall over the face, measure off the right length from the narrower hem up to the edge of bonnet or hat; the middle of veil is to be pinned to middle of bonnet, carrying this middle line over the crown to the middle of back; pin there; this must be done on a person, as it is important to have the front fall to just the waist line, and when draping

131

back have a *straight fall* from brim to waist, not contracted, nor spreading out; then lay plaits backwards; even both sides with an inverted box plait down the

FIG. 15—PARISIAN TURBAN FOR SECOND MOURNING

back; this gives the best effect; the sides should be so plaited back that the front corners fall gracefully just back of the shoulders, and that there is sufficient ease to lift and throw back the veil. (See Fig. 12.)

The draping of veils is an art that must be learned

by study and practice; no amount of telling will teach it; workers should practice on dummy heads with imitation materials till they can get plaits even on both sides, or uneven effects in graceful, artistic lines; this is the only way to learn and succeed.

FIG. 16—NET VEIL WITH CRÊPE HEM

To drape a veil, the hat or bonnet must be firmly pinned on a real or a figure head. Have a distinct design in mind, and proceed to carry it out. Every season some fresh idea presents itself; study these new modes and practice them on imitation materials first, because a few attempts and failures will take all the

133

FIG. 17—CRAPE VEIL, CASCADE EFFECT;
SEPARATE FACE VEIL

crisp newness out of the crape, and it will look mussed when you do get it right. Always find the middle of your veil, baste a line if necessary, and when pinning on a folded veil take care by measurements that both sides are even, and *keep them so*. Pin on and work from the middle to each side, laying each plait the same depth and pressing the plaits, when completed, with the flat hands. It helps to pin the plaits away down and leave them so a while, but use small, fine pins or the marks will show. Use dull head pins to pin on veils, and hide the steel.

Some designs can be pinned flat on the table and then put on the hat; it is impossible to give rules for this; it's like draping a velvet, felt, or Neapolitan hat; one can *do* it, but the how must be learned by practice, as the embryo sculptor learns to mold the clay into form as he *sees* his teacher do; no one can *make* him do it. The writer has often evolved a design from her handkerchief, or any stray bit of tissue paper lying around. You can try the idea in miniature; then carry it out on a larger scale; but do not handle new crape unless sure of yourself.

Periods of Mourning

Mourning for father, mother, sisters, brothers, children, is of crape for the first three months, but the veil need only be worn at the funeral, except for parents, when it is optional to wear it longer; and the entire mourning may be lightened at will, but mourning face veils are correct for three months, and now the black chiffon veil is so much in vogue that many young women wear it from choice. The veil of fine sheer Brussels net two yards long, hemmed with crape one inch wide and several crape folds above, is correct even for a young widow, draped around her crape toque, the ends falling gracefully at the back.

The clever saleswoman has not only to consider the grade of mourning but the style of costume her customer will be likely to wear, this, if she has a good

135

dressmaker, being according to her build and style. If it is any way possible, a call over the telephone will get this important information, so that the headwear may be in harmony with the scheme of the toilette. A knowledge of the correct costuming of the day is a very necessary bit of stock in trade. Your customer should come to you at least every month to have renovations and changes made in her mourning chapeaux.

Net face veils are only permissible in the last periods of mourning, and these must be plain black, without figures other than small dots.

For young ladies picturesque hats are permissible, but for older ladies they are not in good taste, and becoming things can always be found without offending either conventions or art. Small, simple, "smart" hats are to be had in so many shapes that no one need be unbecomingly hatted; and veils long or short are easily draped on any shape.

Here is a little table of periods and grades for depth of mourning, but this is an elastic law, to be modified to suit feelings and tastes, and the prevailing custom of the period or country.

For a widow, crape two years, slight mourning one year (cut in half if desired). Long veil six months, lighter six months.

For father or mother, crape six months, black without crape three months, slight mourning three months. Veil three months.

For son or daughter, if adult, the same as above.

For children, less if desired.

For sister or brother or grandparents, same as above, less if desired.

Uncles, aunts, first cousins, nephews and nieces, crape trimmings only on black. Face veils; no long veils.

"Complimentary" mourning is worn for relatives-in-law, distant relatives, or friends one wishes to honor. This is black and white in mourning combination.

On the length of veils sufficient has been said above,

but we must not forget the widow who has to go out to business after her bereavement; for her it is quite correct to leave her heavy veil at home for state occasions and wear only a thin gauze face veil.

Mourning veils are especially hard for short, stout women to wear; let the saleswoman see to it that the veil is kept in long, *narrow* lines at the back; a toque with good elevation is best for such a woman.

A tall, slim woman may have the lines of her veil falling more about her form, and the woman of medium height with full form should have longer, narrower lines, keeping the veil at the back, and the chapeau small and neat.

Illustrations from photographs.

Fig. 12. Small widow's bonnet, plain covered, with double Alsatian bow across front, formed of folded crape. Veil two and one-quarter yards long, with 12-inch hem at back; front hem 7 inches wide. Draped over front to waist line, back laid in four box plaits.

Fig. 13. Same bonnet. Veil same length, 10-inch hems at each end. One selvedge side is folded over four inches and laid in a deep box plait at the middle, with another on each side; these are pinned against the front bow, forming a wide coronet; the veil is invisibly pinned in easy flutes at the back. This is a very graceful arrangement; a small crape-edged face veil is correct with this; to be carried and pinned under the long veil at the back.

Fig. 15. Parisian turban for second mourning. The brim is of wood silk braid; the wide soft crown of thick peau de soie is draped flat on top, with a couple of raised points at the left back, which is split. A flat strap of folded ribbon crosses the crown, held by two dull jet cabochons; at the back is a full double cascade bow of No. 12 peau de soie ribbon.

The veil is one and one-half yards long by one yard wide, of silk Brussels net, run with peau de soie ribbon in widths Nos. 9 and 5, on a hem four and one-half inches wide. It is draped to the shoulders in front, all four corners falling at the back. It must be so arranged that the ribbon comes clear below the face.

Fig. 16. This is a Parisian second mourning or later dress hat. The wire frame is covered with fine silk Brussels net; the underbrim is faced with an embroidered piece of net, done in dull jet beads and paillette, with raised flowers and leaves in black taffeta and chenille; the embroidery binds the edge. A huge lobster bow forms the top of crown and almost covers the brim, held in front by a long buckle matching the brim. Three large rosettes of the same chiffon taffeta ribbon fill in the back brim, raised by a deep bandeau.

The veil is fine silk Brussels net, edged with crape, the ends falling free at the back. This veil is one and one-half yards long by one-half yard wide.

Fig. 17. This illustrates widow's dressy mourning veil of thin crape or heavy net, edged with heavy crape; fine net, crape-trimmed face veil. The veil is a square of one and one-quarter yards, arranged in cascade on back of toque.

To Renovate Crape

The cleaning houses charge from $3 to $5 for renovating a crape veil, and it is worth it, but they insist on keeping them a week or ten days, and sometimes an order is wanted in a hurry; then it has to be done in the workroom.

Fig. 18 shows the method of steaming a crape veil. Both hands are needed to keep the heavy iron from pressing on the crape.

Unpick the hems carefully, brush the crape well on both sides, pin it out on a table large enough to hold it; if it has to be done in sections, extra care will be needed. Have the table covered with blanket and cloth as for ironing, and pin the selvedges in straight lines true to the edge, and the cut ends also in true lines. Pin closely to the cloth with the pin heads out. Now lay over one end a strip of muslin wrung out of ammoniated water,

138

spread *it smooth, and hold over* this a well-heated iron;
hold it so close that it draws the steam and dries the wet
cloth, but on no account let the iron *press on the crape;*
this would leave a mark that cannot be taken out. When
the strip of muslin is dry, wet it again and place over
the next strip, taking care that each overlaps the last a
little. When all is done, unpin, lift carefully and lay

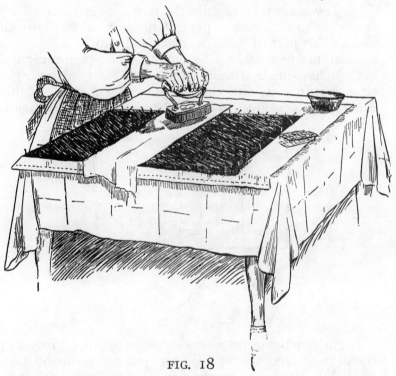

FIG. 18

out flat to dry off; the crape will be crisp as new. Then
hem in the usual way. (See Fig. 18.)

Small pieces can be done in the same way, but care
must be exercised that they are pinned true, not pulled
out of the right run of the threads; this is not quite easy
to do, but if you remember which is straight and which
bias, you will soon find the correct way, and be able to
use up many a bit advantageously.

LESSON IX

LACE TRIMMINGS

Plaitings

PLAITINGS of some sort are always used, and fashion decrees them an extra prominence every few seasons; and as in the writer's experience very few milliners can make perfect plaiting, it will be well to give this part of their work consideration.

Machines now make all kinds of plaitings and ruches, but machine-made trimmings are ruled out in the high-class workrooms, and the milliner who aspires to this trade must be perfect in every detail of hand-made trimmings.

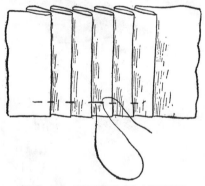

FIG. I—SINGLE PLAITING

Begin practicing on narrow single plaiting (Fig. I); lay all folds from left to right an even depth side by side, or slightly lapping, according to how full you wish it to be; *darn* the needle along; it is best not to draw it out; just push the plaits off the head of the needle as the work proceeds, so that when finished it may be drawn up fuller, or stretched a little if necessary. In sewing take care that each plait receives one or more firm stitches, or the work will spread and break; this is to be observed in all the plaits given. In single plait it is correct to pinch the folds all the way up; the same plait may be sewn through the middle, both edges being finished in some way. The folds may be very fine, or laid deep, whichever seems best for the design in hand.

Fig. 2 shows the simplest form of box plait; it is the same as the previous plait, but every alternate fold is laid the reverse way; all must be of the same size, and

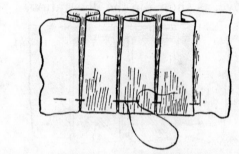

FIG. 2—BOX PLAITING

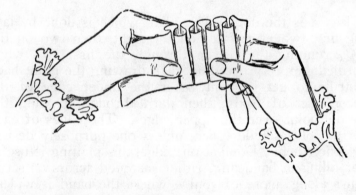

FIG. 3—"QUILLING," SHOWING METHOD OF WORKING

evenly spaced. The second fold may be laid under the first one, which makes "quilling," a very full, effective plaiting; the quills must lie evenly beside each other, as shown in Fig. 3, which shows also the manner of holding the work. These plaits may be sewn through the middle, forming flat ruches.

Figs. 2, 3, 4, 5 must *not be pinched,* but the folds

be kept fluted out, as this is the chief beauty together with perfect regularity of these trimmings, whatever material they may be made of. Only careful practice will ensure this result, holding the work so that the finger tips *only touch the part to be sewn.* No rule can be given for this, as some find it easier to work with the hand *below* the work, while others hold the plaiting with the hand above, as shown in the illustration.

FIG. 4—DOUBLE BOX PLAITING

Fig. 4 is the double box plait, which is done by laying first two even folds on the right, then two on the left, running the needle through the first two when formed, before proceeding, then drawing the point back a trifle to get it firmly over the under edge of the second set of folds; then darn through, passing the needle point over the upper edges. The edges of each set of folds should touch, unless one purposely desires to space them. Done at one edge, this plaiting is useful for filling in bandeaux, either cascaded across or set in rows along, more of course where the band is widest.

FIG. 5—TRIPLE OR ROSE PLAITING

142

It is pretty set up around the crown of a hat, in ribbon, folded or frayed silk, velvet, or several rows of tulle, the base finished with a twist or folds, or slender garland of flowers; or it may be plaited through the middle and used in many ways that will suggest themselves to the trimmer.

Triple plaiting is done in the same way; first three folds laid to the right, and sewn, then three of *exactly the same size* to the left, the folds meeting on each side,

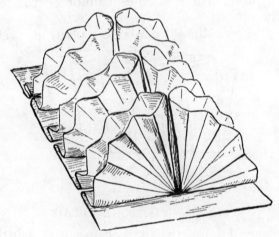

FIG. 6—"ROSE" PLAIT.
A RUCHE OF FOUR PLAITS

so that both sides look alike. But a variation may be made by laying the successive folds a little narrower on the upper side, so that each fold shows a trifle beyond the one above it; in this case each fold is secured with a tiny back stitch, so that once made it is firm. (See Fig. 5.)

Box plaited ruche of four folds to each side is called "Rose" plait because, when finished and sewn on, the upper and lower edges meet over the line of stitches, forming a full rounded ruche. (See Fig. 6.)

Naturally the more folds are laid, the greater care is

necessary; the novice may find it necessary to test each by a bit of card cut to measure, but practice will soon enable her to judge the right dimensions by the eye. In "rose" plait ruches of soft materials it is often necessary to secure each set of upper and lower plaits by a "tie-stitch" a little in from the edge, so that the round effect will be secured and retained; this "tie-stitch" is just a pick-up tiny stitch tied in a firm knot and the ends cut close; it is the invariable method of securing trimmings in place, where stitches cannot be carried from one to the other.

Fig. 7 shows the "Fish-bone" plait, a pretty full

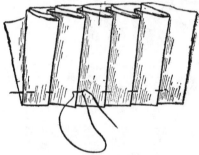

FIG. 7—"FISHBONE" PLAIT

ruche, placed last on the list because it is a little more difficult to achieve—and to describe. It is the one ruche that is made so well by machine that its use is pardonable, but as frequently one cannot get it in a required color or width, it is most necessary for the milliner to be able to make it. It is, in fact, a single box plait, but the shape and laying of the folds produce the V-shaped effect; by studying the detail line cut a better understanding of the following instructions will be obtained. Begin by laying a fold to the right, next one the other way, but instead of laying it beside the first, as in Fig. 2, lay it *around* the first, so that the under edge of fold 2 comes even with the edge of fold 1. Now lay the second plait by allowing it to extend, however, on the left back—follow the line diagram—then fold under again, making fold 2 meet the edge of fold 1, and so continue. *The left edge of all folds are pinched*

FIG. 7A

DETAIL OF FISHBONE PLAIT

thus:— < < < which gives the effect peculiar to this trimming. Two rows laid against each other make a handsome ruche, or several rows set up against each other are most effective, in tulle, mousseline or light crisp silk.

FIG. 9

SHELL TRIMMING FLAT

FIG. 10

SHELL TRIMMING DRAWN UP

"Shell" Trimming

This pretty and useful bit of work may be made of double tulle laid in a fold an inch or more wide, silk folds, double or single, with edges frayed or stitched, ribbon in various widths, velvet, of course, and wide

145

soft braids may be drawn up in shells forming a decorative change. Fig. 9 shows a silk band run with matching silk. Fig. 10 shows the same drawn up into the shell effect. It forms pretty edges; or sectional trimmings between plain folds or braid; done in wider ribbon, with a wire sewn under, it is used in odd pretty bows in various ways. It is very pretty in crape or silk for mourning.

It is not the trimmings themselves that make the beauty of any chapeau; it is the art with which they are used and applied. Remembering this, let the milliner look on these lessons as helps by the way; there is not a

FIG. 11—WHIPPED FOLD, FLAT,
SHOWING STITCH

FIG. 12—WHIPPED FOLD,
DRAWN UP

season that something new does not appear, and the milliner's experience in what she *has* done will enable her to successfully handle every new thing, no matter how intricate or difficult it may appear.

Whipped Folds

Fig. 11 shows an especially pretty and novel method of making full tulle folds, used only on the best chapeaux, however, by reason of the work and care required in their making. Whipping is a stitch frequently employed in our work, for lace, ribbon, etc., but in this trimming the *stitches show,* and form the decorative upper edge of the fold, as well as answering the purpose of drawing it up. The method might be applied to narrow ribbon or bias strips of frayed silk, mousseline de soie for mourning hats, etc.

Fig. 11 shows the fold flat with the stitches in progress. Fig. 12 shows the same drawn up ready for use. For an example, cut the tulle strips 2½ inches wide, fold over and shir the two edges together, leaving the thread as long as the work, *i. e.,* flat. For the whipping, use crochet or embroidery silk to match, or contrasting if this is desired. In a slight mourning hat the black tulle may be whipped with white, or *vice versa,* and delicate touches of shading may be given by having the silk a shade or two different from the folds. The tulle is fulled up on the whipping thread (and the gathering thread, which is the same length), quite full, certainly three, or possibly four, times the length required, and it must be good, crisp tulle. When a length is run, the two threads are drawn up at the same time, holding the fulled part firmly under the flat hand, and evening the fullness afterwards. When finished it results in a flat, full fold, with decorative silk thread edge.

The uses of these folds are various; they can be applied to cover entire brims; a charming bonnet is evolved from them; mounted on foundations of fine cape net, or stiffened tulle, they trim "collars" around hat crowns; or they are set round tulle wings and quills, finished by narrow folds, or jet trimming. They are run on strips of plain tulle double, and made into unique rosettes and ruches.

Lace Bows and Other Trimmings

Like all other special features, lace bows get their turn on fashion's wheel once in so often; they are very beautiful when rightly managed; otherwise they have

147

an inconsequent, dowdy look. A large bow of black French barb lace, or piece lace cut and edged with scalloped insertion appliqued on, is very handsome; it must, of course, be upheld by wire; this should be fine lace wire to match, buttonhole sewn in, in the same way as directed for wiring ribbon; the lace must be held quite easy, so that it will not make a ridge when the loop is formed. When lace wire is not at hand, double silk covered spool wire, or even the wire stripped out of "taste" or tape wire (the best silk kind), may be used. Large loops may have a hem run at the edges and the wire run in, turning the end of wire over so it will not catch in the lace.

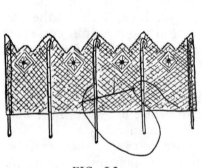

FIG. 13
WIRING LACE WITH BRACES

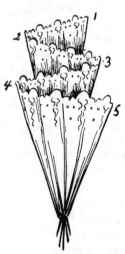

FIG. 14
LACE COQUILLE,
FINISHED

Lace, when used to form brims, coronets, etc., where the wire inevitably shows, must be wired in line with the scallop or design, from ½ to ¾ of an inch from the edge; fine silk or thread must be used, and the buttonhole stitches should be not more than ⅛ of an inch long. Occasionally it is necessary to work the wire into the *edge* with an ornamental blanket stitch. In this way the lace may be shaped to any form.

Lace butterflies, flowers, quills and wings for the hair are wired with spool wire set a little from the edge, and if necessary following the pattern; of course, in no case may the stitches show on the right side. Laces for the hair frequently have a spangle or bead sewn in on the wire with every stitch, or gold or silver covered wire is used.

Lace coquilles can be made of lace from 4 to 6 inches wide, set up with "braces," which are uprights of brace wire, buttonholed on *across* the lace, the upper point being turned over and firmly sewn just below the edge of the lace; when gathered up at the base, these braces are covered by the flutes of the lace. (See Figs. 13-14.)

Economy in the Workroom

In this connection it is apropos to say that there need be no waste in the workroom if piece boxes are kept for the various kinds of materials, and these turned into all kinds of pretty, useful trimmings and ornaments, which is acceptable and interesting work for the apprentices and improvers during the dull seasons.

From cuttings and remnants of lace one can evolve butterflies, wings, quills, lilies, tulips, wild roses, pansies, etc., and leaves of various kinds. Cut the patterns first in paper, shape wire by these, and sew this with small blanket stitch to the lace, then cut round; finish the edges with narrow lace, spangled trimmings, or bind with ribbon or velvet. Odd bits of aigrette, or sprigs of fern or flowers, come in here nicely, as also odd bits of narrow ribbon, which can be wired and spangled and formed into little rosettes to finish the lace ornaments, or into dainty "spider" bows, with bits of fern or aigrette. Nice bone hairpins should be sewn on the under side of these ornaments, and flat brooch pins, sold for this purpose, on corsage ornaments, which are often required to match those for the hair.

Scraps of silk and chiffon may be turned to use in various ways, made into blossoms for the same purpose as the above, mounted with foliage for hair and corsage ornaments, or made into petals to mingle with the petals of roses or violets, in flower chapeaux. Button ornaments of silk, laid over with spangled lace, are pretty as centers to rosettes, and can be made of "scraps."

Approximate Quantities Required for Plaitings

Single plaiting, 3 to 4 times required length.
Single box plait, same.
Double box plait, 5 to 6 times.
Triple box plait, 6 to 7 times.
Four-fold or "Rose" plait, 7-8 times.
Fishbone, same.
Whipped fold (tulle), 3 to 4 times.
Shell trimming (silk), 1½ to 2 times.

LESSON X

SIMPLE BOW MAKING

THE making of various kinds of bows is only a part of the uses to which ribbon may be put. Like other materials, it is the means of expressing the artistic ideas of the designer; hence the chief thing to learn is the dexterous handling and light manipulation of ribbon; this acquired, will make the carrying out of any design an easy matter.

Ribbon is never out of fashion, but some seasons it is made a prominent feature, and "bows" of all shapes and sizes are used as the chief trimming on nearly every shape, the character of the arrangement being designed suitably to the shape of the hat or bonnet, and suitably for its purpose of wear.

Wiring Bows

The very rich stiff ribbons are set up without wiring, but even they will flop when taken into wear; the best plan is to wire long loops while making the bow, and invisibly "tie" the shorter loops to these, so all will hold their pose. Fig. 1 shows wire loops bent up to lay into the loops of ribbon, the join at the base coming in the "waist" of the bow, but if this is to be straight up and

FIG. I—WIRE LOOPS

down, each wire loop must be cut separately and laid in, folding the ribbon over quite loosely, so that no sign of wire appears outside. After the bow is made, the loops are secured inside with a couple of "ties." The "Quill" bow (Fig. 2) is made and wired in this way; a similar bow is shown on the hat (Fig. 3) with a pair of long wings added.

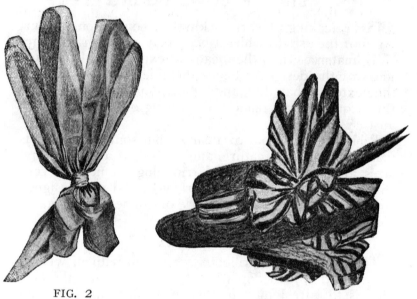

FIG. 2
QUILL BOW WIRED   FIG. 3—QUILL BOW POSED ON HAT

There is another method of wiring ribbon for bows of a different style, as shown in Fig. 4; in this case the wire, which should be a fine, rather soft size like lace wire, and, if possible, match the ribbon, is buttonhole sewn on the wrong side of the ribbon, along the middle or nearer one edge, according to the kind of bow to be evolved; only one thread of the back web is taken up with a fine needle and silk to match, the stitches being from one-half to one inch long. Begin sewing at one end, holding the ribbon straight before you, and work *towards* you, throwing the thread to the left under the thumb, which also holds the wire in place, the needle passing under it as shown in the illustration; when the loop under the thumb is released and the thread pulled, the tied stitch is formed; this method takes just half the time as making the buttonhole stitch with two movements. In sewing hold the ribbon *easy* and the wire straight.

As matching wires are not always at hand, a box of water colors and brushes should be part of a milliner's equipment, so that she may at a moment's notice be able to color her wire and thread to the desired shade; they dry quickly, and only as much as required need be done. The same plan is used to get matching frames.

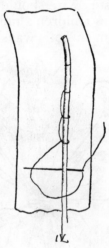

FIG. 4—WIRING RIBBON

Fig. 5 shows a bow wired in this way, each loop and end being bent into quaint curves and twists; the shape of this bow varies; it may be large or small, but the ribbon is never wider than two and one-half inches, and it may be made of the narrower widths. It is variously called a "Marquise," "Antoinette," "Cupid," "Spider" and "Watteau" bow, each of these, however, having its own little variation; the construction is the same, but the number and size of the loops vary, also the width of the ribbon. The best way to learn these distinctions is to go to a good gallery and study the pictures of various periods, though this style of bow belongs to the artistic

153

time from immediately before till some years after the Directoire and Empire period. One sees these pretty bows woven in tapestries, decorating exquisite wall papers, carved in the wreaths upheld by cupids on picture and mirror frames, and inlaid in colored woods on the beautiful furniture of those days. All and everything beautiful of art can be a help and an inspiration to the milliner who knows where to look, and how to make use of what she sees.

Ribbon or "taste" wire should not be used for setting up bows, except in children's millinery, where it is preferable; it is put in in both ways described above. Rib-

FIG. 5—MARQUISE BOW WIRED

bon wire is also used to sew into hems of ribbon, which is to be bent into waves for a trimming around a crown; there its soft flat nature is most appropriate. It is also useful as a foundation on which to mount a succession of short loops to form a wreath or plume, the loops being sewn on one at a time as they are made. (Fig. 15.) Ribbon wire is often split up, the individual wires only being used to wire tucks in ribbon for shirred rosettes, "Sunflower" bows, "feather" bows, and a number of devices where a soft support is best.

Let it be understood that no bow or rosette must *look* wired; the supports are merely a means to an end, and must not even be indicated.

The bow (Fig. 5) is in one piece of ribbon; beginning with the short lower end, two upward loops are formed and these firmly twisted at the waist with tie or flower wire; next a second downward loop is laid (behind the end), then two more upright and tied, then the third downward one and tied; now one twist around the waist, and the end *sewn* in place upward. The quirks are put in last, and the loops may be spread or set up at will. There are here six loops in all; by putting three up and three down alternately a different shaped effect is obtained, and by making the loops larger and rounder the "Spider" bow results, which in No. 9 or No. 7 ribbon velvet is a characteristic trimming on one of the large "Watteau" shapes; in red with poppies and buds tied in, in blue with bluets, in pink with roses, etc., etc., there is no end to the charming combinations to be had. Made small and slim, it is pretty for a

FIG. 6—METHOD OF HOLDING BOW IN MAKING

bonnet, with aigrettes tied in with the loops, the same making a smart hair ornament; even fine ferns, lilies of the valley, etc., are tied in.

Ribbon is so easily mussed, if gathered or plaited up wrongly it is almost hopeless to make a nice, fresh-looking bow of it; it is therefore wiser for the novice to practice first on strips of tissue paper, then on cheap lining cambric, till the fingers have acquired dexterity and assurance in handling. Notice in Fig. 6 how the loops are formed by the left hand and laid into the "waist," which is held by the right hand, *i. e.,* to twist the tie-wire round, or sew, the whole thing is transferred to the left, then back again, for the next loop. It is quite possible to hold several yards of ribbon thus between the fingers without a single tie or stitch, the final tie-knot alone holding the entire structure, as shown in the large "Fan" bow (Fig. 14), which contains five yards of ribbon, but this particular model was made of the same measure of tissue paper, cut four and one-half inches wide.

FIG. 7—SIMPLEST TIED CRAVATTE BOW

It is prettiest to begin a bow with an end, and after the tie-knot leave an end as finish; but if the ribbon is single-faced and very slimsy, ends make the bow look poor; then see to it that the gathered ends are well secured, so they do not work out.

To go back for a moment to the wiring with loops: If you look at Fig. 6, you will see how easily the loop of wire can be held within the folds of the ribbon at the waist with the right hand, the left hand bringing the ribbon down over it; downward loops need no wire, and the next supports are laid into the succeeding upward loops.

Fig. 7 shows a "Cravatte" bow, which is the simplest form of bow, tied from one piece of ribbon, beginning with an end, then a loop opposite, then a loop the same side as the end, next a knot over the waist, which must be so tied that the second end comes opposite the first.

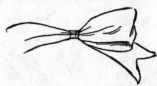

FIG. 8—DETAIL OF TIED LOOP

Fig. 8 shows an end and loop tied with fine wire where the loops are all to run one way rather flat, each loop being laid back and tied in the same way; such a garniture is used on narrow bandeaux, around crowns, and as a cascade or flat wreath effect running obliquely over deeply turned-up brims or down crowns.

FIG. 9
DETAIL OF
ROSETTE BOW

FIG. 10
SIMPLE RIBBON ROSETTE
OR "CHOU"

Fig. 9 is the rosette bow in the making; gather the end of the ribbon, or lay it in plaits if a more "crushed" effect is desired, and sew firmly; make a loop the size required, and gather down on the stem already made; hold a pinch of the ribbon next this stem firmly between

157

thumb and finger to form the stem of the second loop; pass along the needle or wire and twist round the stem without pulling, so that the pinch space is left clear, as is shown in the illustration. This is necessary to get a good effect when the loops are sewn together at the base or arranged on a foundation, be it a bandeaux or disk, such as is shown in Fig. 11.

Fig. 10 shows a rosette made of loops as described,

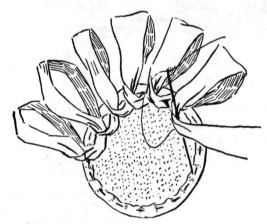

FIG. 11—ROSETTE ON FOUNDATION

eleven of these being sewn together by turning the two end ones into the middle and arranging the others round; each is then sewn to the next at their base underneath; such a rosette would take 1½ yards of 4-inch ribbon; more and deeper loops make a larger "chou."

Fig. 11 shows a rosette being made on the foundation, which is of cape net wired round and bound with head lining ribbon. The ribbon used is a No. 5 velvet; the process is clearly shown, each loop being laid up and sewn, then brought backward with a circular swing and sewn down with a forward slant, when the end is again folded upward and sewn down for the next loop. A second, third and fourth row are set round, filling the disk to the middle; this is a handsome rosette,

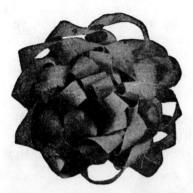

FIG. 12—DAHLIA ROSETTE
OF NO. 2 RIBBON

FIG. 12A—DETAIL OF
DAHLIA ROSETTE

In narrower ribbon a wider swing backward, giving
an almost round ring effect to the loop, makes a very
pretty rosette, called the "Dahlia" (Fig. 12), and another way is to make the loops of No. 1 or 2 ribbon,
almost flat, which makes "chrysanthemum" rosettes.
Rosettes, like bows, are of an endless variety, and the
milliner who takes a real interest in ribbon trimmings

FIG. 13—BACK VIEW OF HAT. SIX DOUBLE LOOPS
KNOTTED ALL IN ONE PIECE ON BANDEAU

will find ideas come thick and fast once she gives her
artistic ability full sway.

159

If one is not quite sure of the quantity of ribbon required for some design to be evolved, make it up in paper cut the width required; this is especially wise when buying expensive ribbon for some special order; it takes only a few minutes and assures a fresh successful bow without hindrances.

Fig. 13 shows the back view of the smart sailor hat. A succession of bows consisting of one loop up and one down, each having its own tie-knot, are set along the

FIG. 14—FAN BOW. FIVE YARDS RIBBON, UNCUT

bandeau, which is 2½ inches deep at the middle back there are six of these bows; the ribbon is all in one piece, being carried from one bow to the other. The entire trimming of the hat took 5 yards of 5-inch ribbon.

Fig. 14 is a "Fan" bow composed of five yards of ribbon 4½ inches wide, all in one piece; unless this bow is rightly held and built up, it will not acquire this shape. It is commenced at the base by leaving an end or loop to the right; the loops are laid alternately *back and forth*, not up and down; a single faced ribbon must be twisted so that the surface always remains outside; a double faced ribbon does not need this twist. The length of the loops is gradually increased towards the center, all being held between fingers and thumb of the right hand, the loops laid with the left, and wire loops laid in if desired in the four or six middle loops; the tie-over is formed *up and down* in the middle of the bow, just a tight slim twist, *not* a tie-knot, but wire should firmly tie the waist before the tie is put over; then the last end is sewn in place on the back and "tied" to the loops. The same style bow in narrower ribbon and fewer loops can be made; this model was used on a hat with high sloping crown, and with the exception of a twist of tulle,

FIG. 15—AIGRETTE BOW

and flowers on the bandeau, formed the "feature" of a very stunning hat; it was posed against the crown at the left towards the back.

Fig. 15 shows an "aigrette" bow suitable for the front of bonnet or toque; the high loops are wired and the downward ones made very short and "crushed," a very tight waist being tied with wire, and when the loops are all made one or two real knots are tightly tied around the stem, so the crossed part of the knot comes outward. This bow takes about 1½ yards of 4-inch ribbon, or 2½ of No. 16.

Soft wide ribbon, wired or not as may be indicated, is pretty with a decided twist made in each loop; this gives rich shadings very effective in some colors. (Fig. 16.)

Wire loops are "tied" inside ribbon loops by picking up a couple of threads of the under side of the ribbon and tying the thread securely over the wire.

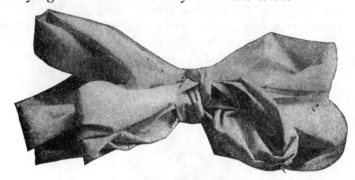

FIG. 16

"Wreath" Effects

Entire wreaths and rosettes are made of short *crushed* loops set close together. (Fig. 17.)

FIG. 17—"WREATH" OF NO. 16 RIBBON, CRUSHED LOOPS ON RIBBON WIRE FOUNDATION

Fig. 17 shows a pretty ribbon trimming made on a foundation of ribbon wire. It is best made in soft *crushable* ribbon; the loops are laid alternately to right and left, but each overlapping the other a little, so no space is left down the middle. The ribbon should be

162

plaited down onto the foundation, firmly sewn, then turned over to the other side, sewn, and the next loop formed, plaited, sewn down, etc.

This is charming to catch up brims, trim bandeaux, and in narrow ribbon makes pretty wreaths for the hair. Made of wider ribbon and larger loops it is pretty around crowns. It may be made of two shades of the

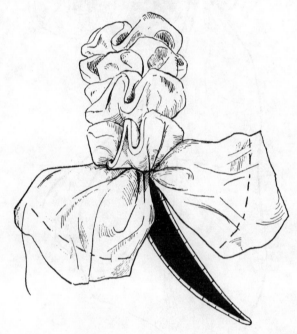

FIG. 18—TRIMMING OF TWO SHADES OF RIBBON, CRUSHED LOOPS ON BUCKRAM FOUNDATION

same color, one on each side, or alternating by crossing the strands.

In Fig. 18 is shown a similar trimming made of two shades or two different colors of ribbon; it is made on a buckram or cape net foundation, wired; this also is pretty for bandeaux or to catch up brims, or on a straight foundation, around crowns; any width of ribbon

FIG. 19

FIG. 19—ROSETTE OF CRUSHED RIBBON
LOOPS ON FOUNDATION

may be used; if a "crushed loop" effect is desired, plait
the ribbon instead of gathering it.

Fig. 19 shows a rosette made in the same way, but
here one shade at a time is used, the second being set
inside the first row; the inner loops should be a little

higher to give a pretty round effect, like the half of an orange.

Pretty and effective rosettes are made by laying even loops alternately to each side, as many as desired, and simply tying the waist with wire and setting the loops up; such rosettes may take from two to four yards of ribbon.

Then there are ribbon trimmings when a bow or some other arrangement is constructed to be posed on one part of the hat and the ribbon carried over and again "tied" on another part; many yards of ribbon may be put on one hat *without* cutting.

As before observed, there is no limit to the ideas to be evolved; the chief thing is to learn the quick, light and *assured* handling of ribbon; then nothing will be difficult or intricate.

LESSON XI

DRAPING

IN every business, trade or profession, whatever may depend on the cleverness of the brain, the genius of the mind, in whatever manner it may find expression, that is ART, and is inborn; it must be there or it cannot manifest itself; no one can teach this; we can only show ambitious students how to use the materials and tools, by means of which the beautiful ideas they hold within themselves may find expression.

This is just as true of the artist-milliner as it is of the sculptor or painter, and the beautiful effects that may be obtained by "draping" a piece of material come under the class of artistic manipulation. It may be in you or it may not; only by making the effort to do something can you discover this talent. Therefore, try.

Given the same size and shape of piece of velvet in the hands of a dozen persons, all working on the same shape, copying a draped model, no two will be alike, and probably not more than two will be anything like the original.

Parisian milliners will take any odd cutting of velvet, silk or lace, drop it over a frame, a few light touches, and behold an arrangement of beautiful curves, graceful lines, and lights and shadows that tempt a painter. One can readily understand how difficult such a model is to copy; until it is pulled to pieces one does not suspect that it is just a remnant from a gown or mantle! It is therefore not the material that ensures success; it is the deft fingers, guided by the artistic brain.

Draped Effects Over Wire Frames

Draperies must never look as if *sewn;* whatever stitches are necessary must be quite invisible; not only this, but there must be no draw nor pucker that could suggest stitches.

Draped effects should therefore always be made over
wire frames, covered with tarlatan, to which the folds
and puffs can be pinned inside the frame; then, when all
is satisfactorily arranged, tiny stitches may be put where
the pins catch, carrying the needle from one to the other
where practicable, or securing the arrangement with invisible "tie" stitches, where it cannot be sewn. "Tie"
stitches have frequently been mentioned in these lessons,
but we will say for the new student that these are tiny
"pick-up" stitches which are tied in a firm knot and cut
off, not carried along as in sewing; of course, these
must be equally invisible.

FIG. 1—TURBAN BRIM GATHERED ON WIRE RINGS

FIG. 2—SAME SET IN PUFFS ON FRAME

"Mob" crowns, Tam o' Shanter crowns, and every
other kind of crown that is not plain covered, come

under the head of draped crowns. In brims there is a wide range, from the piece of bias material simply swathed around, to the brim first shirred, then draped or "set" into some desired arrangement, such as the turban brim of Figs. 1 and 2, the first showing the velvet shirred on a wire ring at each edge, the second showing it set into points around the flat, turned-up brim. This requires fully double the flat circumference allowed for fullness.

FIG. 3—TOQUE DRAPED FROM 1¼ YARDS OF VELVET

Fig. 3 is done with 1¼ yards of velvet on the straight, but one corner is cut off on the true bias, the long straight side being brought on the left; therefore the velvet must be folded to get it thus. This corner is cut in half, and the selvedges joined on each side to make the piece wider; cut the selvedges off, join by machine if possible, and flatten out the seams. They come under the brim and are not seen, but this addition enables one to get the required fullness on the top, which is arranged first, pinned and tacked, then the remainder is turned under in convenient folds, carried into the headsize as flat as possible, there sewn to the covering muslin, and the surplus trimmed off. The hat when completed with a deep bandeau on the left is really a draped toque, although made on a flat wire sailor shape. You will notice that there is a distinct effect of four lines from edge of crown to edge of brim; there is, of course, no rule about this; one deep fold at any given point may be broken into two, these again into four, and then restored to the one, or the process may be reversed; neither can any rule be given for placing material on frames, except that the bias lines should predominate, and if an elevation is desired at any special point, the widest scope of the piece should be allowed for this. Tight straight folds or lines are to be avoided, and easy curves and gracefully flowing lines worked in. The work and effect are equally good on a small mushroom shape.

Practice in single-face canton flannel in place of velvet, sateen in place of silk, and cheap cambric or net for lace; the inexperienced handling of good materials destroys their freshness, which no steaming or pressing can restore.

A Draped Brim on a Mushroom Frame

Fig. 4 is a draped brim on a mushroom frame lifted by a deep bandeau, which is optional, however. The

FIG. 4—DRAPED EFFECT ON STRAIGHT OF GOODS.
LINES CONVERGING AT BACK

material employed was silver gauze overlaid with several layers of brown tulle; the crown is covered plain, with a bit of sheet wadding under the brown tarlatan which covers the wire frame. In this model the material is used on the straight, one selvedge being run around on the under edge of brim, turned up and arranged in the desired folds, which in this design all converge at the back, where a suitable trimming was posed. The under brim is faced with pink China silk, over which is brown tulle draped in, breadth by breadth, in folds, till four breadths have been used; these are first pinned, then tacked, using a "straw" needle and OO silk, sliding the needle under the silk and taking tiny stitches in the tulle. Of course, the folds may be first made and then run on the foundation silk, or any other underfacing that is suitable may be employed. (See lesson on Shirrings and Folds.)

In this draping when finished two corners are left to be cut off as the circles gradually lessen from edge of brim to crown line; if a bias material is used, one end will be right, the other will have to be joined out, so that both edges are the same, *i. e.*, shorter at the edge that comes next the crown.

It will be noticed that the folds are more raised on the left; they are deeper and one less than on the right. This makes a handsome trimming on a felt or Leghorn hat, in which case the edge is not carried under the brim edge, and the crown left to show more.

These three models have been selected for practice for beginners as they offer distinct classes of drapery, either of which will be found useful in many variations, and once mastered will enable the student to handle most designs she may meet.

"Mob" Crowns

"Mob" crowns are big loose puffs of silk, velvet, or lace (this over silk or other material), gathered or plaited around the headsize, and usually swathed round at the base with ribbon, folded silk, or velvet, tulle, or flat bands of fur, feather trimming, or a flat wreath of flowers. The puff may or may not be drawn down in a

few places into dents. Tam o' Shanter crowns are put
on in the same way, but are flattened on top; one side
may be turned up with trimming, or the garniture may
be tucked under the overhanging folds.

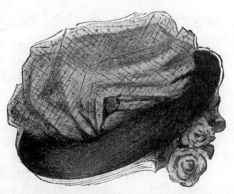

FIG. 5—DRAPED PUFFED CROWN

Fig. 5 shows a puff crown of silver net over one of
stiff taffeta in shell pink, the brim being of dark brown
velvet; only a couple of handsome pins seemed to hold

FIG. 6—TAM O' SHANTER OR "BERET" CROWN

the draperies near the front; the brim, being saucer-
shaped, was underfaced with the taffeta and folds of
brown tulle; the roses that trimmed the deep bandeau

171

were in tonings of brown and pink. This crown can be done in velvet equally well, and would, like Figs. 3-4, be handsome in crêpe or thick mourning silk. A full yard square of material is used in this crown.

Velvet "Tams" With Lace Brims

Fig. 6 shows a Tam o' Shanter crown of velvet on a brim of lace bound with velvet. Clusters of ostrich tips trim each side, flowers filling in the back bandeau, which, however, runs all round. A round cut from a breadth of velvet makes this crown. It is gathered around the edge, set on with only enough fullness to get the flat effect in front, all the remainder being thrown into three deeply set-up waves at the back. The headline is finished with a "French" fold of the velvet.

Figs. 7, 8, 9, 10 show a group of draped trimmings in velvet, silk, or ribbon, which are all suitable for either felt or straw hats. Fig. 7 is of bias velvet, two half-yard breadths being used. One is roll hemmed and

FIG. 7—SIMPLE DRAPED TRIM-
MING WITH BOW

arranged around the hat as shown; one corner, however, is joined out from the second half-yard; the remainder is cut in two, giving $\frac{1}{4}$-yard pieces; the two selvedge ends are mitred, the rest roll hemmed. This forms the simple bow in front.

Fig. 8, if of wide ribbon, has two strands draped

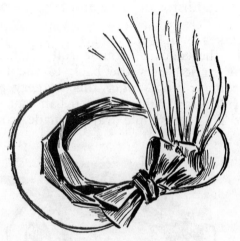

FIG. 8—SIMPLE DRAPED TRIM-
MING, FOLDED BOW

easily around the crown; the simple bow comes a little
to left of front, the tie-over coming from inside the
crown, apparently catching up the brim, which is, however, firmly sewn in place first. This can be done in
silk, using a breadth on the straight around crown, and
the same—a breadth to each side—for the bow, with
half breadth for tie-over. Velvet should be used on the

FIG. 9—ELEGANT DRAPED TRIM-
MING WITH BUCKLE

173

bias, a ⅜ breadth for drapery and two ¼-yard breadths
for bow.

Fig. 9 takes two ½-yard bias breadths joined under
the buckle, the edges of course roll hemmed; the two
points are carried over the back to the headsize, the
feathers coming from under this drapery at the back.
Tulle in full puffs trims the deep bandeau.

Fig. 10. This is a simple drapery made from a straight

FIG. 10—SILK DRAPERY WITH "CHOU"

1½ yards of plaid taffeta; one end is laid in several plaits
under where the wings are placed, then carried round
in graceful lines and curves mostly on the brim near the
crown, so that what stitches must be taken may be done
from inside. The end is formed into a "chou" arranged
after the wings are posed and firmly sewn. In working,
the selvedges can easily be turned under, but if a bit
shows here and there it is no detriment.

Puffed "Chou" and Trimming

To give a better idea how a puffed "chou" is made,
we refer the pupil to Fig. 11, which is made from a
round piece of velvet 16 inches in diameter; this is gathered round the edge, drawn up and sewn on a wired disk

of net 3 inches in diameter; it is sewn around the edge flat, so the wire comes inside the puff. The piece is then arranged in even puffs, the shape rising towards the middle; the puffs are caught to the net foundation with pins, till all is satisfactorily arranged, then sewn with a tiny stitch in the velvet or silk, carried from one to the other on the under side. These "choux" may be large or small, and one can, by careful piecing, use up odd remnants in their make-up that would not make any other nice trimming.

FIG. 11—PUFFED "CHOU"

Fig. 12 is a trimming made from a half yard of velvet on the bias, roll hemmed all round, and drawn down in gradual puffs in the same way as the "chou," but the foundation used was a bandeau 1½ inches wide in the middle, 6 inches long, running to points at either end, and slightly curved. This makes a handsome trimming with which to catch up a brim to the crown, or for a back or side bandeau; it may, of course, be made smaller at will, but does not look well with the puffs too shallow.

As before observed, draping is so much the work of the *artiste* that we can only suggest and encourage the ambitious beginner to practice; she will see speedily if or not she has the right talent, and if so she has a much-prized gift.

FIG. 12—TRIMMING IN "CHOU" PUFF EFFECT

LESSON XII

TRIMMING

HAVING learned the "making" of hats, we come now to the trimming, which is the finishing touch given by the artist milliner, and to which all that has been done before is merely preparatory—a setting, as it were, for the final achievement. This is that part of millinery that cannot be taught. It has been truly said, "Artists are born, not made," and it is just the same in the field of millinery art as in any other of the artistic professions.

But one may have a great gift and not be aware of it; we never know what we can do till we try, therefore let every one make her best effort. First copy the best designs obtainable; study "lines," "pose," "elevations," combinations of color, combinations of materials; the last two offer a vast field, and will bring out the true feeling of taste—good or bad. Lines change, as shapes change with the seasons; but no matter what the fashion of the hour, the lines of *beauty* do not change, they are as varied as the faces of the human race, but in every face and every fashion harmony of line can be found.

Beginners make the mistake of overloading, thinking by the quantity of trimming to achieve a good effect, while a simple piece artistically posed is in better taste and gives the indefinable something called "style."

Feathers

To pose ostrich plumes and tips gracefully is in itself a great achievement; and the milliner will not waste her time who takes an assortment of these of various lengths and modes of curl, and practices their arrangement in various ways on different shapes. She should make herself familiar with the various kinds of feathers, and never mix these on one hat (if it can be avoided). In the best grades this is not difficult, but

177

in the cheaper grades the effect of the finished feather as it looks in the salesroom is the only consideration, and choice is limited, and therefore these should be only purchased as needed for use, while good feathers are always good stock.

One often sees feathers sewn on a hat, absolutely without any definite idea, they sprawl every way, and a breath of wind sets them whirling like the branches

FIG. I—BUTTON HOLE SEWING
WIRE ON QUILL OF FEATHER.

of a tree, wild and hideously unbecoming. These same feathers, put on in harmony with the lines of the hat, and so "anchored" that they will hold their pose no matter how the wind may blow, would produce a beautiful effect. This must be studied and practiced,

178

Wire Supports

Often one desires to give a plume or tip a pose that it cannot retain without some support, then we have recourse to wires. One way is to buttonhole sew a fine firm wire matching the feather on the underside of the quill, cutting it, however, before the tip or "head" is reached, so that this may fall soft and loosely. (See Fig. 1.) The wire should be firmly secured to the stem at the root of the feather by twisting tie wire or strong thread around; this firmly sewn to the hat, the wire can be bent into a raised curve and when "anchored" at the head end to the hat wherever it may touch it, will keep its curve, but it may also need a "crutch." This is a long or short loop of wire placed under the deepest part of the curve, secured to the quill of the feather by a few strong "tie-stitches" and sewn to the side of the crown at the other or cut ends of the loop; tulle, ribbon or other trimming passing over this. The crutch is used also where the quill is not wired, and is often quite enough support. (Fig. 2.)

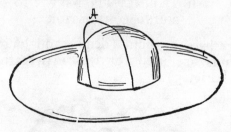

FIG. 2.
SHOWING "CRUTCH" WIRE "A"
ATTACHED AT BASE OF CROWN

The "Prince of Wales" tip requires a wire to keep it upright if the stem is at all soft, and as the under side of this (except the head) is curled over to form the front or face side, the wire must be secured to the back, turned in a little loop when the head is reached, and secured with several firm buttonhole stitches. This

179

tip from the nature of its treatment is used for up-right poses only, small ones for bonnets, medium sizes for toques and the larger sizes for hats; but these are only occasionally seen. (Fig. 3.)

FIG. 3—PRINCE OF WALES TIPS TRIM-
MING BONNET, FIRST SEWN TO
ROUND FOUNDATION

For large hats, medium (demi) and long plumes of various kinds are used; or tips in wreaths (Fig. 4) or clusters (Fig. 5).

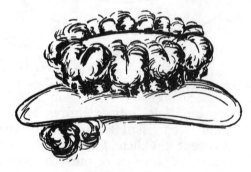

FIG. 4—TIPS SEWN TO CROWN
IN WREATH EFFECT

FIG. 5—CLUSTER OF TIPS, WITH LONG
PLUME SEWN TO FOUNDATION "A"

Foundations

When feathers or tips are to be posed from one point
it is best to sew the entire arrangement to a small foundation, and then sew this to the hat, usually against
the crown, but occasionally one wishes the feathers to
start from the brim, either some place on a flat brim,
or the edge of a turned-up hat, in such case the foundation must be made so that it will fit the place where
it is to go and be no larger than the trimming, or
ornament that must cover it.   Fig. 6—A, B, C, D.)

These foundations are of buckram or stiff net, wired
round the same as bandeaux, and covered with the same
velvet or silk as the hat; after they are sewn on, some
trimming must be carried over, or another bit of velvet
twisted over to hide the feather stems.

In transparent hats, or very delicate straws, where
there is practically nothing to sew to, a similar piece,
but only covered with lining silk, is held inside the

181

crown and the other carrying the feathers is sewn to this. The same support is useful in very fine felts, chenille, crinoline and other fancy braids, and silk or velvet hats made over wire or net frames.

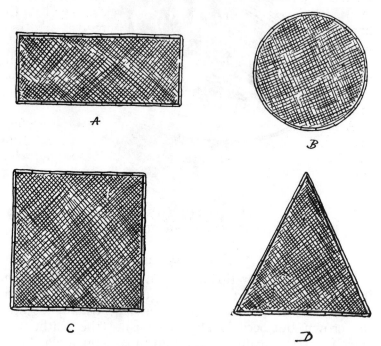

FIG. 6—FOUNDATIONS FOR MOUNTING
FEATHERS. A, B, C, D.

Posing and Sewing on Feathers

When sewing on feathers, pose and pin first with large bead head, or blanket pins, no others will hold, and remember that pinning never gives as graceful effects as sewing; when the arrangement is satisfactory sew each feather stem to foundation, or hat, with a few but very strong stitches.

To "anchor" feathers to a hat (a term coined to describe method), we employ long or short "loop" stitches, that is, a needle with double or strong thread is passed between the stems of feather forming its quill; for feathers are usually made of two or three single feathers laid on each other, or if single, the thread is firmly tied on the under side of the quill, then secured to a point in the hat that will hold the feather in just the right pose, neither too close against the hat, nor too far away, and the loop thread is tied in a firm knot and cut off.

When the feather really touches the hat, the needle is passed from the under side of the quill into the hat, then back up the other side of the quill, and there tied in a tight knot and cut off.

A charming method of supporting feathers where practicable, is to arrange one or more puffs of tulle matching the feathers under them, and if necessary letting the tulle conceal supporting wire loops.

FIG. 7—FAN EFFECTS, SEWN ON
FOUNDATION "D"

Wings, Breasts, Etc.

Wings are of two makes, either they are "natural" or "made." The first is as its name implies, just as it is taken from the fowl, cleaned, dyed and dressed, and is strong and stiff, often needing to be almost broken to get an effect of grace. Such wings look well on stiff "tailor" hats, and for children are really the only sensible wings to use.

"Made" or manufactured wings are of many shapes and change with the fashions. As these are made of feathers glued on foundations they are more or less fragile; still the best made are fairly durable. As a rule these have an upper and under side, and unless the foundation is wired, or one wishes to use them flat, they will need to be wired on the under side. This must be carefully done, using fine strong wire, buttonhole sewing it on, and carefully lifting the little feathers with the needle to pass the stitch beneath. Begin at the root of the wing, leaving a couple of inches of wire for a stem, bend the wire into a loop that will

FIG. 8—WIRE LOOP ON WING

nearly reach the edge of the lower or broad part of the wing, twist the wire around the end left in beginning and secure the two together with tie wire; then sew down the loop. (Fig. 8.)

By the wires the wing may be bent and curved to fit

into the place it is best suited to occupy; but in bending care must be exercised not to split the feathers, and when sewing on, the stitches must be invisibly placed between or under the feathers; the stem being sewn very securely as directed for ostrich feathers.

Entire birds are usually manufactured, and the long trimming needle is easily passed through the soft body; but here, too, the rule applies, that *stitches must not show,* and no part of the plumage may be pulled down so that stitches are even suggested; use as few as possible, but let these be strong and well hidden.

Breasts of birds are either the natural dressed skin with the feathers left in, as in grebe, peacock, pheasant, duck, grey or white goose, gull, etc., or they are manu-

FIG. 9
FOUNDATION FOR MOUNTING
A BIRD'S BREAST

factured by gluing little feathers on a foundation of muslin; these last are always ready for use, but the natural breasts sometimes need attention.

Of course these skins have a great deal of oil in them, which, unless they are properly cured, causes them to retain a disagreeable odor, and the oil will presently soak up to the plumage, causing it to look stringy and worn. The fresh pelts should be thoroughly rubbed with salt and arsenic, stretched on boards to dry, and then well cleaned with naphtha to destroy any remaining odor. When perfectly cured such breasts will last indefinitely and are far handsomer than the made imitations.

But before using the natural breasts they must be mounted on foundations made of fine French stiff net, cut to size and shape and wired round leaving the two ends for a stem (Fig. 9), or lapping them as in a bandeau. On this foundation a bit of wadding is basted, and over the other side a bit of lining silk is laid, the edges turned over and caught over the edge of the wadding; the breast is then sewn to the foundation with an invisible stitch among the feathers near the edge and slip-stitches in the silk; it can then be bent to any curve desired.

In using made breasts, one needs to exercise care or the sewing will break off the little feathers; if any come off, they must be replaced by touching the underside of the root with glue and setting in place with a pair of tweezers.

In handling quills, sew the *end* of the quill firmly, and take care not to split the fine flue, as that would ruin the quill.

Curling Feathers

Feather cleaning, curling, and of course dyeing and making, is a business by itself, and takes a long time to acquire, but every milliner should know enough to keep her stock of feathers in good order, or in an emergency clean or tint a plume.

FIG. 10—FEATHER CURLING
KNIFE

The feather curling knife (Fig. 10) is the only tool

186

needed; if the feather has become stringy shake it for a few minutes over heat, or hang it in sun and breeze, then, beginning at the top, pass three or four fronds between the edge of the knife and the thumb, as shown in Fig. 11; let the pressure be light from the quill out to near the end, then press more firmly, this will turn the *ends under* and not narrow the width.

If the quill is very thick it is prettier to hide it a little by lifting a few fronds over it by curving them up and back with the knife near the quill, from each

FIG. 11—CURLING A FEATHER

side alternately; this is done by a deft turn of the wrist, the knife held above the fronds instead of under them. Look at a well curled feather and you will see at once how this is done.

The "head," or tip end of a feather, is curled so it looks full and fluffy, only one or two fronds at a time are taken on the knife and the pressure must be very light. Heavy pressure gives a kinky curl, which is ugly, and also the pressure must be *even throughout,* so that all the ends may be curled over a finger, or curling stick.

To make a Prince of Wales tip the fronds are so tightly curled towards the *under side* of the quill that it is hidden. The stem is bent flat, except the head which droops over sharply from the top. (See Fig. 3.)

"Lobster" or "snake" plumes have the fronds curled over towards the upper side of the quill, which necessitates passing the under side over a hot iron (not *too* hot) to straighten it out, and reverse the curve.

The cleaning, tinting, etc., of feathers is treated of in the special article on renovation generally.

FLOWERS

The arrangement of flowers is so much the work of the artiste designer that rules cannot be given, but the mechanical part of the work has its best methods.

Nature is always a true teacher; when we find her isolating one set of blossoms, and gathering others into clusters, we may safely follow her guidance in the disposition of the artificial presentments, as also in the selection of ground colors for the grouping of various blossoms.

It is never in good taste unduly to crowd large blossoms on a hat; give each its full space to display its beauty, and let the arrangement of the whole be so harmonious that one single leaf removed would be missed. On the other hand, there are small blossoms like violets, small heartsease, forget-me-nots, and the like, that require full grouping to ensure the desired effect, the foliage being here rather a setting for the flowers, than a part of the whole; and yet, the blossoms without foliage would be unnatural. Often this conventional treatment is, however, a distinct note of the season's fashion. We see close set, line straight wreaths of flowers, with an equally stiff wreath of foliage as a complement, this being a seeming defiance

188

of all Nature's laws, but in a suitable setting, the effect is good and artistic.

The combination of large and small flowers demands artistic skill. Take, for example, a large rich Burgundy rose, making the center of a bouquet of violets, lily-of-the-valley, and mignonette; unless the red and purple are of just the right shades, it will look crude, but artistically combined it is exquisite. Such combinations cannot be taught, the artistic sense must be cultivated until the perception is mentally true to art in its highest sense.

Some flowers seem to suggest youth, while others are more suitable for the wear of older women; we do not put pansies on a child's hat, or buttercups and daisies on the hat of an elderly woman, yet rose buds may be correctly employed to trim hats or bonnets for any age.

Flowers should be sewn on with as few stitches as possible, but these in very strong thread, not in continuous stitches but at the several places where the spray, bunch, or single flower touches the crown, or other convenient place; but large heavy flowers must be securely sewn at the end of the stem close against the flower, and may need a couple of stitches in the lowest layer of petals.

When sewing a circle of roses or other large flowers around a hat, each one must be laid in its place and separately sewn; but a wreath of smaller flowers is made first, then "tied" in place as before directed.

Bouquets or flowers may be sewn to foundations the same as directed for feathers, but these are more often made of wired cape net, and a bit of tulle twisted over after the stems are sewn down; this depends entirely on the nature of the hat, however.

To make a wreath of flowers cut a green wire the length required, and bind the blossoms and foliage onto this with the finest green tie wire; arranging them as the work proceeds. Rubber tubing slipped on bare wire stems of leaves or blossoms greatly improves their appearance and value.

Flower Hats

Flower hats are made by sewing the blossoms flat on a frame previously covered with crêpe Francaise or tarlatan to match, and over this a loose layer or two of tulle, which forms a soft bed for the flowers, and obviates the necessity of crowding. Usually the stems are cut off, and the flowers sewn on flat by the undermost layer of petals; but sometimes the stems, if very pretty and good, are carried up, or down, and used in some decorative way; as, for instance, carried up and laced in basket effect over the crown; or carried from the crown down and run over the brim.

Foliage hats, or crowns, are made by sewing the leaves on a green tulle bed, by their lowest points against the stem; this secures both the leaf and the wire that runs under its middle, and every leaf must overlap the next a little, but too much regularity should be avoided. If different sized leaves are used the smaller should go towards the crown. Use green thread if possible, as silk slips; and fine matching thread for flowers.

Supporting Flowers

In posing upright arrangements it is often necessary to introduce a "crutch," which in this case is a *close* loop of green wire (or black, white or purple as the need may be); twist the cut ends in with the ends of the blossoms, and "tie" the heaviest, or those desired, upright to the support with bits of green tie wire. Sew the whole firmly to the hat.

Ribbon Trimming

The making of ribbon trimmings has been fully explained in another lesson, and it is only necessary here to add a few general directions.

Usually a bow or other ribbon trimming is first made, then sewn on the hat, but occasionally the ribbon receives a new character by being arranged in bow form, *on* the hat. This again is the designer's work, though ordinary bows are often made by the "maker" if she happens to be clever at this branch of millinery art; in fact, one finds at times a very clever bow maker, who was absolutely a failure in any other part of the business. This is a period of specialization, and it is not unwise to work out to perfection any special branch in which one finds oneself to excell.

Sewing Bows on Hats

Bows, when required to be the chief object in the decoration of a hat, should be pinned first with large bead-headed pins and tried on; when the pose is right as regards the shape of the hat, it must be securely sewn *underneath;* not a stitch may show, the folds and flutes being absolutely undisturbed; this is very important, then if the loops are long they must be just as invisibly "tied" in position, so that no matter how the wind may blow they will remain in the position you design for them.

The sewing on of feathers, flowers and ribbon trimmings all has this one rule,—as few stitches as possible, but these very strong and *quite invisible,* and equally invisible "ties" to hold various parts in place.

The Use and Arrangement of Lace

There are so many kinds of lace that when one speaks of a lace hat the first question is. "What kind of lace?" In high priced hats only real (hand-made) laces are used, and are often cleaned and re-modeled to newer designs, but lace is so much the vogue for all kinds and prices of millinery, that the manufacturers are continually trying to bring out closer imitations of the real laces, and with such success, that many almost defy detection by the uninitiated.

In using the heavier laces, such as Irish, Renaissance, etc., or any thing that has a distinct motif or pattern, it is not well to have the lace on both over and under brims; the wire frame is first covered with fine silk or cotton net, according to the lace used, and the lace laid on this smoothly; if the shape is eccentric and the lace will not come smooth by stretching, it must be clipped and the pattern laid over so that when finished it looks as if the lace were made to the shape of the hat; which in real lace is often the case.

The under-brim, covered with net, tulle folds, shirred tulle or net, or mousseline de soie, is filled in to the head. The crown is overlaid with double net, and the lace put on, rounding the edge, and fitting the side in the same way as directed for brim. This is for piece lace, but there is another way to use this, no covering being laid over the frame, but the wires bound with baby ribbon, narrow ribbon velvet, or chenille, or the lace tape, of which the inexpensive Renaissance lace is made. Then the lace is laid on the upper brim, secured to the edge, which is finished by a ruffle of lace, tulle, flowers, or a band, which may be of velvet, silk, or metal tissue. The wires of the crown are not covered.

Lighter laces such as point Appliqué, Alençon, Chantilly, figured Brussels, etc., either in web or edge widths, may be used both over and under the brim, the edge finished in any way that seems appropriate, and rarely need any previous covering over the frame, unless the edge lace is very sheer, and is to be slightly full, in which case a covering of double tulle, both under and over, will be necessary. No rule can be given; the milliner must in every case be guided by the nature of her materials and its purpose, the under coverings being merely an accessory to improve the effect of the lace or aid in its arrangement.

Laces that are to be fulled can be drawn up by a strong thread usually woven straight into the straight edge, if there is not one a thread should be *whipped* (not run) in.

Point d'Esprit, Brussels, ring net and tulle are very dainty, and may be trimmed with ribbon and flowers; and those of silk net or tulle with feathers.

LESSON XIII

THE MAKING OF RIBBON AND SILK FLOWERS

FLOWERS and blossoms of many kinds can be reproduced in ribbon of various widths, mingled and mounted with the stamens and foliage of the ordinary artificial flowers, but this is a branch trenching so closely on the business of artificial-flower making that it needs time and practice to attain proficiency. It is profitable work, used more for hair and corsage ornaments than hat trimming.

There is, however, one way in which a knowledge of this work can be put to profitable use in the workroom; that is to use up scraps of silks, gold and silver tissue, crêpe, lace and ribbons of all widths, to make pretty trifles for the hair, etc., during the dull season. All these materials may be used double and if possible on the bias.

Lace, however, can be used singly, the shape of the petal outlined in fine lace wire, or silk-covered spool wire, the lace edge turned over this, run in and finished with fine straw braid, chenille, spangles, or narrow lace edging.

Petals of net or mousseline de soie from scraps used thus, spangled all over, and edged with tiny lace, make charming flowers, pansies, wild roses, camellias, etc., the outside petals of course being larger than the central ones.

Each petal is tied with a bit of tie wire; then, beginning at the center, they are arranged and tied together so all the stems are underneath in one bunch. If a long stem is needed, the central petals are tied to a wire, and the rest around it, the end finished by a twist over of the material of the flower. Wings, quills, butterflies can be made in the same way; the shape is in wire, the material laid on flat, cut to shape with one-half inch margin; this turned over and sewn under the wire, some trimming covering the sewing.

The best education is *observation* and *study;* and if you see an effect that is good, practice it till you make it your own; we all have the privilege of learning from others, and let us work so well that others may find something to learn from us.

The vogue for ribbon and silk flowers has grown considerably in the past few years, and as pretty hair and corsage bouquets and other decorative effects are a profitable adjunct to a millinery business, it is well to know how to make them in the workroom, this being pleasant work to give apprentices during the dull seasons, and a means of using up odds and ends.

Roses and buds, lilies, daisies, violets, "forget-me-nots," dahlias, asters, sweet peas, pansies, carnations, sunflowers, in fact, a great many flowers, are possible of charming reproduction from scraps of silk and ribbon. The few specimens shown in this lesson will suffice to give any intelligent student the key to the production of others, taking as models real or well-made artificial flowers, or copy the pictures to be found in any good gardener's catalogue; and much useful help may be found in a good book of directions for making paper flowers, especially as regards the accessories, such as the calyx, etc., but the wires must be finer and the foliage better than such as are used for paper flowers.

Ribbon Flowers

Materials necessary for rose sprays, rose centers, cusps, calyx, rubber tubing, spool fine uncovered flower wire, skein green filloselle silk, green covered wire, two and one-half yards of pink, white, or yellow satin ribbon three inches wide, one and one-half yards of two-inch to match. Rose foliage, one bunch of three sprays is enough for a spray of two roses and buds.

To Make the Roses

For the largest rose, cut five lengths of the three-inch

194

ribbon, each five inches long; double over and gather the two cut ends together, inserting a loop of the wire, cut five inches long, so the two ends of the wire come below the ribbon; draw gathering thread up tight, twist a few times around wire and fasten off. Make the five petals thus:

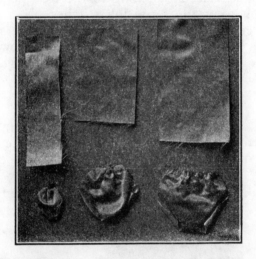

3   2   I

ILLUSTRATION I—THE WORK IN DETAIL

Cut four lengths of the two-inch ribbon each four inches long; make four petals in the same way as the larger ones. Roll the two corners of each petal over and "slip-stitch" down. (See Ill. I, Figs. 1, 2, 3.)

The petals are now ready to put around the center; take up one at a time of the smaller ones, tie them to the central wire with tie wire, just a couple of twists to each; place so each overlaps the other slightly; next tie on the larger ones. The curled-over side may be turned towards or away from the center; it looks very natural to turn a couple of the outer ones away. Bring all as close up to the stamens (rose centers) as possible, then slip on the calyx (i. e., the little green leaf star at the base of roses); now cut a length of tubing to slip over the wire stem, and over this slide the cusp, the little wax cup that finishes the rose.

The foliage can be tied on with green raffia or tie wire, but may also be slipped into the tubing by piercing this at any desired point.

The calyx will need fastening to the rose petals with a speck of photo paste or invisible stitches.

If rose centers are not at hand, center the rose by making a bud as directed further on; or a yellow center can be made with yellow baby ribbon, tied in tight knots as directed for "forget-me-nots."

Half-Blown Rose

For this use three of the two-inch and four of the three-inch ribbon petals, curving them over the center, except one or two petals, so the center shows only on one side.

ILLUSTRATION II—THE FINISHED ROSE

Rose Buds

Around the top of the loop of wire (cut five inches long and doubled over) twist a bit of white wadding; cut a piece of the two-inch ribbon two and one-half

196

inches long, cut this in half lengthwise (See Ill. I, 3),
place the wadded loop of wire in the middle of one strip,
the finished edge upward, and fold the ends toward the
middle till they overlap, forming a pointed little almond-
shaped cone (Ill. XII). The ends can then be securely
wired onto the central wire; calyx, tubing and cusp
added, as for the roses.

It is pretty to make buds of various sizes, by adding
from two to five petals of graduated sizes. The flow-

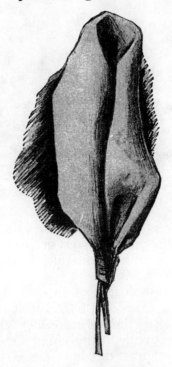

ers and foliage are then arranged and tied to a firm
wire, encased in tubing, with green tie wire, raffia, or
the green floss silk. (Ill. II, Finished Spray; also Ill.
XIII.)

Button and cabbage roses are made with narrower
ribbon, with a tiny bud center; the petals do *not* have

the corners rolled back, and are all curved towards the center, lapping each other. (See Ill. XVI.)

Full blown roses have the petals all turned away from the center, and are improved by using two shades of ribbon, the darker for the larger petals.

ILLUSTRATION III—FINISHED DAISY SPRAY

Daisies

For a spray is needed 10 yards of No. 2 white or yellow satin ribbon, six yellow or brown button centers (on wire), one bunch suitable foliage, or fern; tie wire, tubing, floss silk.

Measure three-quarters of an inch, and tie a knot in the ribbon (Ill. III, Fig. 1), twist it so the right side comes uppermost, measure another three-quarters of an inch and secure with the end to the base of button with tie wire, repeat the knots, and tie the petals to wire so they form a flat star; if a double daisy is desired make a second row under the first, making the knots at one-inch lengths. From six to twelve petals are required according to size. Now slip on the calyx, which is unlike the rose, being a flat disk, with pinked out edge (there is no cusp); secure with the photo paste and slip on the tubing.

198

The buds are made on the wadded wire loop. Tie a two-inch bit of ribbon in a knot around the middle of another two-inch bit, secure the knot to top of wadded wire by a stitch, bring the four strips down over the pad and secure to the wire with tie wire, slip the calyx over this, snipping it three or four times from the edge to near the middle, so the sections will lap and secure with photo paste, twist the rest of the stem with green silk, beginning and ending with a tied knot. Larger buds are made by using more bits of ribbon, tying all at the middle with one knot.

Wire to a firm wire, introducing the foliage, with silk or tie wire.

Violets

Of No. 2 satin ribbon 10 yards in the preferred shade, violet foliage, orange sealing wax, tie wire, green or purple raffia.

Cut as many bits of tie wire five inches long as you require violets, double in half, twist a tiny loop in the top, and on this drop a bead of the sealing wax. Some slip yellow glass beads on and twist to hold firm, or a double knot of orange silk. Measure a half inch from end of ribbon, tie a knot (Ill. IV. Fig. 1), twist the ribbon on both sides of the knot, form the petal and twist to beaded central wire, the same as for the daisy, continue round as many petals as desired, and a second row for a double violet, this having the petals three-quarters of an inch; be sure to twist the ribbon. This is the difference between the method of making

199

daisies and violets; in the former the ribbon is kept flat, the latter is twisted to get the crumpled petal effect. From four to six petals are enough for a simple violet, two to three for buds. (Ill. IV. Figs. 2 and 3.) Wind the green silk closely around the base of the finished flower; this forms a cusp. (Ill. IV, Fig. 3.) If green stems are desired, continue the silk to the end of wire; if for mourning, make center of white wax or bead, and wind stems with purple raffia or purple silk. Mount the finished flowers with the leaves in the same way as before directed, or in a solid bunch.

ILLUSTRATION IV. FIGS. 1, 2, 3
BUNCH OF VIOLETS AND DETAIL

Violet Buds

For these cut as many lengths of wire as desired, making a quarter-inch loop in the end; twist a bit of wadding round; cut two bits of ribbon each one and one-half inches long, tie a knot around center of one with the other, fasten on top of loop, bring the four ends down over the pad, *twisted,* and secure to base with green silk. Slip on a round calyx, snip same as for daisies, and paste to bud; very little of the violet shows.

The paste should be put on with the tip of the little finger. Spiral buds are made by twisting one strand of ribbon over a closed loop of wire, with one petal at base. If you desire soft stem buds or violets, use purple rubber or muslin tubing, and secure this in suitable length over the short wire stems, wiring the soft stems in place to the bunch; or double knots may be tied in four-inch lengths of ribbon and these wired in, but they do not look as natural. The bouquet is much improved if tied with a yard of No. 7 ribbon to match, in a couple of long loops and ends, and the collected stems encased in silver or purple paper.

ILLUSTRATION V—RIBBON SPRAY OF FORGET-ME-NOTS

"Forget-Me-Nots"

Blue No. 1 ribbon, 10 yards; skein of green filloselle; tie wire and suitable foliage; maiden-hair fern being the prettiest. Measure off two dozen lengths of tie wire five inches long, slip a pink bead, or make a pink silk knot on the double middle. Measure off one-half of an inch at end of ribbon, make a tight knot, repeat knots at every three-quarter-inch space till you have four (see Ill. V), fold the petals in a cross, pass the middle of wire loop with bead over center and twist underneath; bend upward, and secure the two cut ends underneath with the green silk, beginning and ending with a tie to the end of the stem.

The buds are made by tying the ribbon in a knot on the loop, twisting it down over the wire to a depth of half an inch, then finishing with the green silk. Some spiral buds may be introduced. To mount, tie flowers, buds and foliage in pretty grouping on a firm green wire, with green silk, or green tie wire; lay on one at a time, tying neatly and firmly. (Ill. V. "Forget-me-not" Spray.)

Flowers may be suitably perfumed by putting a bit of good sachet powder in the wadding of buds, or between the double ribbon or rose petals, or by laying the materials for a few days in a box with sachet powder.

Silk Flowers

Silk pieces for flowers should be on the bias, and of thin material, but taffeta, on the straight or bias, can be used for some blossoms, either using the selvedge as one would ribbon, for sweet peas, pansies, orchids, etc., or the edge finely pinked out or frayed, as for carnations, and similar blossoms.

For silk roses the material should be on the bias, and of thin make, as it is used double. If the strip is long enough, it may be run to form the petals, but

ILLUSTRATION VI
GATHERING SILK FOR PETALS

short bits can be gathered into single petals and wired on to the central stem.

The bias strip, measuring from three to six inches across, is folded over edge to edge and gathered, as shown in Ill. VI, the petal being twice the length of its depth; this is for the inner petals, the wider is shirred in straight lines, as is Ill. VII; the threads are later drawn up from end to end, and the petals arranged and secured to the rose center by fine tie wire,

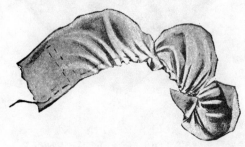

ILLUSTRATION VII
STRIP GATHERED FOR OUTER PETALS

around the ragged end. The length of each petal should, for the small ones, be at least twice the width, and three times this in the larger petals.

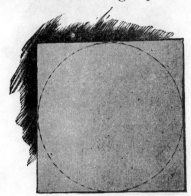

ILLUSTRATION VIII
PIECE OF SILK FOR BUD CENTER

If you have no stamens to center the rose with make it of a three-inch square of silk (Ill. VIII), which may be the same as the rest, or of a deeper shade, or even a yellow center in a pink rose; indeed several shades of pink may be used in one rose. In arranging the petals lap them slightly, except the outer ones, which may be curved back. To return to our center; gather a circle in the square (Ill. VIII), insert a five-

ILLUSTRATION IX
FIRST FOLD FOR BUD CENTER

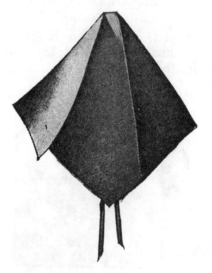

ILLUSTRATION X
WIRE LAID IN BUD CENTER

inch loop of wire with a bit of wadding twisted on,
(Ills. IX and X), draw the thread up tightly, and
wind the petals around this center. A variation of
this is to gather a four-inch square as before, then
having secured the four points to the wire, draw the
puff down by a few stitches in two or three little
puffs. (See Ill. XI.) This gives the effect of a just
opening rose; such a center should not be yellow,
however, but deep rose in a pink rose, slightly yellow
in a white rose, and deep orange in a yellow rose. This
is also the center of some buds.

Small buds and centers are made by folding the
square in a triangle (Ill. IX) with the wire loop inside,

ILLUSTRATION XI—PUFFED CENTER

folding both sides over (Ill. X) and over again (Ill.
XII), then with tie wire securing the points to the
wire, a closed calyx is slipped on, secured with photo
paste to the bud, a tiny cusp comes next, and a bit of
fine rubber tubing puts a neat and suitable finish to the
bud. Pretty moss roses and buds are made by substituting the feathery sea fern for the calyx, pasting

several bits of this on the petals, wiring on at the base,
then putting on the cusp, etc.

Buds of various sizes and degrees of openness are

ILLUSTRATION XII—BUD CENTER

made by wiring on few or more petals of suitable
sizes. (Ills. XIII and XIV.) In using single petals,

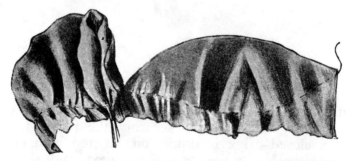

ILLUSTRATION XIV—BUD CENTER LAID IN PETALS

hold the ends firmly and secure each with one twist
of the wire only, till a circle of them is in place, then

A CABBAGE ROSE

ILLUSTRATION XIII   ILLUSTRATION XV—LARGE
LARGER BUD   BUD CENTER

SPRAY OF RIBBON ROSES AND BUDS

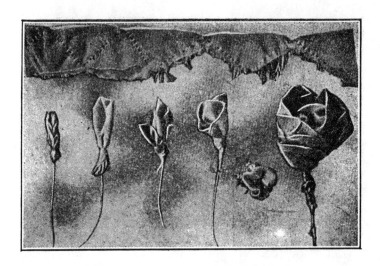

BUDS AND DETAILS OF VARIOUS BUDS IN RIBBON

DETAIL OF BUDS AND CENTERS

SILK ROSES; BUDS, AND DETAIL

add a few twists more, avoiding any clumsiness in construction or untidiness in finish.

If one has neither calyx nor cusps, the first can be replaced by bits of green silk cut out to shape, or narrow ribbon or silk gathered and set on; and a cusp can be made of green sealing wax, molded around a thick wire, first wetted or greased, as it will then pull off.

Ingenuity in devising pretty conceits is a great gift, but quite capable of cultivation and well worth while, for the profits to be realized from the "piece box." Not only odds and ends of silks and ribbons, laces, velvets, etc., but old flowers will often yield the calyx, stamens, cusps, wire, etc., for use in making the flowers.

Carnations

As before observed these can be made of straight, or bias silk, pinked out at one edge in tiny points; if a pinking machine is not at hand, snip out with sharp scissors. For a large flower three strips are used, measuring one and one-quarter inches wide by six inches long, one and one-half inches wide by seven, one and three-quarters by nine. These are gathered in rather large stitches an eighth of an inch up from the straight edge (the ends being also pinked out); the threads are drawn up tightly around a central double wire loop made of a four-inch square of silk drawn down in little puffs as directed for rose bud center (Ill. XI); and each successive ruffle, beginning with the narrowest, is tied tightly below the button close up against each other. Calyx, cusp, and tubing complete the flower.

The calyx and cusp for carnations are different to the rose variety, and in making buds the center shows little; half open buds have just a little frill or two breaking out between the long green points, and the foliage is also quite different; it is essential to get the correct accessories, or imitate them cleverly in silk or ribbon. Maidenhair fern is made with No. 1 green ribbon, fine brown tie wire and green filloselle. Knots form the leaves, with a tiny loop left above each, the wire being hooked in the knot, the ribbon cut off and neatened with the silk, beginning and ending with a tie. Use a bit of the real fern or well-made imitation as a model.

Dahlias

These can be made of silk or ribbon. If of silk, it may be on the straight if there is a selvedge, if on the bias it must be double. In either case this flower, as also the sunflower, is best made on a round foundation, in size from one and one-quarter to two inches in diameter. The petals are made and sewn on singly, beginning at the edge and working round and round to the center, letting each row lap the previous one, one half; the center may be finished by a crumpled puff, a circle gathered round drawn together, sewn on and drawn down in little puffs by a few stitches from underneath.

ILLUSTRATION XVII
SWEET PEA

ILLUSTRATION XVIII
MAKING SWEET PEA PETALS

Several shades of the same color can be used in these flower rosettes. The petals should be cut from one to one and one-half inches wide, and double this in length; they are then folded twice from each side to the middle (much as is done in Ill. X of the rose buds), then the base is sewn in a quarter-inch space on edge of foundation.

A dahlia rosette may be made of three-inch ribbon thus: Allow seven inches to each petal, lay a triple box plait, with *center inverted;* beginning at the upper right hand edge, plait *across* the corner, along the lower edge, and again up across the left hand corner to the edge, plait closely, and sew to foundation in a one-inch space, repeat till the foundation is encircled; thus if the disk is four and one-half inches in circumference, you should have five petals; allowing for the lost bits between petals one yard of ribbon will be used. Another row round of narrower ribbon (may be of lighter, or contrasting shade) will make a handsome flower; the center can be filled with little crushed loops. Dahlias of No. 7 or 9 satin ribbon have each petal cut, used flat, the ends of three to four-inch strips folded over twice towards the middle so they meet and are sewn down as before described. Two or three widths of different shades of the same color make a handsome flower, the lighter shade being in the center.

Sweet Peas

These also can be made of ribbon or silk. If of silk, it must be on the bias; the back petal is made like a

ILLUSTRATION XIX—ARUM LILY

rose petal, the central one like the folded bud from square (Ill. XII) and the two side petals like the smaller rose petals, each wired to the stem coming from the central bud. A small calyx finishes these blossoms, with suitable foliage sprayed in. (Ill. XVII. Finished Sweet Pea.) Two or even three harmonizing shades, and colors may be combined; look at the real blossoms for models.

If narrow ribbon is used the back petal is single, gathered at the base and up the sides, the center made on wire as before described and the side petals double as for a ribbon rose with *one* corner curled over and slipstitched; wire and finish as before directed.

Arum Lilies

These are little used except as table decorations at Easter, but are made of wide satin ribbon or bias silk, folded as for a large loop, drawn down and curled back as for a large rose petal, the ragged ends wired around a single stamen, made by twisting wadding around a stem of thick satin wire, and around this winding No. 1 yellow velvet ribbon, winding up from the base then down again so every bit of the foundation is covered.

LESSON XIV

TAKING STOCK—CAREFUL PACKING AWAY —RENOVATING MATERIALS

TWICE a year, at the end of each season, every workroom, as well as the stockroom, should have a thorough "house cleaning." If account is taken of stock, as it should be, not once but twice a year, not one least item should be overlooked, and everything, when measured, carded neatly, or laid smoothly in its original folds, with plenty of tissue paper between, as this prevents creased folds becoming permanent or cracking.

Velvet, silks, net, and other web goods should be brushed with a good hair whisk; feathers, wings, birds, etc., must be lightly brushed, and when put in newly

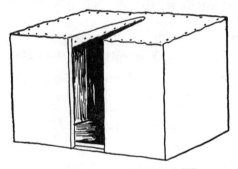

FIG. I—STEAMING BOX

papered boxes, several bits of camphor put among them.

Flowers and foliage must also be brushed, but a rather stiff inch-wide paint brush is best for these; then the leaves must be smoothed out, crumpled petals smoothed, and if necessary attached to the flowers with a speck of white photo paste.

Ornaments must be brushed with a small stiff brush, like a fine close tooth brush, then folded away in tissue

paper. If steel shows any rust, brush with powdered
rotten stone, and burnish with leather.

If stones are missing from any good pieces, it costs
but a few cents to have them replaced, and so retain
their full value.

If feathers need cleaning or recurling, leave this till
you need them for use; there are fashions in the curl
of feathers, you know, and, besides, they go out of curl
laying by, almost as much as if out in the case.

Felt braids and feltings are not only beloved of moths,
but bugs will get into the folds if not well protected; a

FIG. 2—BOX WITH IRON READY TO DROP

thick layer of cedar and camphor dust under the tissue
paper is a good preventive, and has no offensive odor;
the same applies to felt hats.

Straw braids and hats, if put up on high shelves,
where it is dry and hot, will crack to pieces; put them
as near the floor as possible, but avoid damp, as that will
destroy the colors.

Tulle and veiling nets also crack with dry heat; and
made wings, birds, and breasts will fall to pieces, the
glue drying and cracking.

Flowers and foliage, too, are made largely with glue,
and must therefore be kept in a cool but dry place. It is

215

a good plan to keep maiden-hair fern flat between two cards; and other fine foliage, if arranged between ropes of tissue paper, will keep in salable condition; indeed, flowers should never be crowded, but so arranged that they look *new* until sold; "stock well kept is stock well sold" is one of the truest sayings, and another is that "there's nothing to waste in millinery."

No matter how old things may be, if well kept their turn will come again. A hat manufacturer had several large cases of expensive hair and Tuscan laces which year after year were taken in stock at less and less, till the sum was nominal. Then came "new designs from Paris," and he realized on that lot more than their original value.

But in going over the stock much will present itself that should be sold at once, even if at a loss. Such things should be put in the workroom and made up in the most attractive way; thus, with ingenuity and good taste, all odds and ends are made into salable, profitable hats and bonnets, and marked at "sale" prices.

If there has been a specially popular color during the season, and one finds oneself rather overstocked, create a demand for things in that color by an unusually attractive display both in style, value, and price, and "unload" this stock. The same method is used in any line of hats of which there are many on hand; trim a lot, all differ-

FIG. 3—BOX WITH IRON DOWN IN PLACE

ent, and use up on these all the odds and ends of the season's stock, mark them at a small profit, as "reduced" goods, and if they are tasteful and fresh they will sell.

Clear the shelves as much as possible for the incoming stock.

In selecting the goods that must be cleared out, remember that feathers, real laces, good velvets, silks, silk and velvet ribbons, and many other items, are staple goods, and need not be sacrificed; but although you may remove a valuable feather from a hat and replace it with flowers or a handsome bow, it will not pay to rip off bows of very expensive ribbon and replace with new inferior quality; a very costly ornament or flower may be changed, and a scarf of real lace replaced by a less costly one, but all this must be done according to the judgment of each milliner, who will know how far her trade will pay for value received.

Many high-priced milliners do not go to this trouble, because the prices they get during the height of the season cover the loss on stock not sold till the "markdown" period.

But it is to the milliner who must count every dollar, and get the full value of all she buys, that these words of help are directed.

Having taken account of stock, we are in a position to know what we will *need* to start the next season, and how far we may indulge in the addition of some of the many novelties that always tempt one. Buy very carefully of these; feel your way; public taste is so fickle and does not always prove to coincide with your own; leave a margin for the pretty novelties that each week of the season brings out, but of staples have as good a selection as your purse and your trade permit.

Among novelties we may class very eccentric shapes; a few well selected will soon show if they please your trade; then get more; but simple shapes in the hands of a clever milliner can assume the most modish lines; such shapes are preferred by all Parisian designers, as they

217

can bend and twist them in so many and varied "lines of beauty."

A clever milliner who understands the possibilities of her materials and the use of her tools—her brain, eyes, and fingers being chief among them—will be able to evolve pretty attractive chapeaux from the odds and ends, the "left-overs" of the season's work, even shopworn and soiled trimmings being cleaned, steamed and freshened for the "mark down sale" rush.

Felt hats after being brushed may be further cleaned with a bit of crape for black, or very dark colors, and white book muslin or thin crinoline for light colors. Suede kid is also good.

Straws after brushing may best be cleaned with a bit of velvet over the tip of the finger, and if the paper lining is torn have it replaced. Weed out for sale all extreme or "novelty" shapes, as these would be recognized as "old style" next year, and if any have to be carried over let it be the simple shapes.

Put both straws and felts away in wooden boxes if possible.

If hats with bows have to be packed away, fill every loop with a wad of tissue paper, and support lace ruffles, flowers, feathers, with light ropes of paper, so they will come out fresh and salable.

This, by the way, is also necessary when goods are to be shipped by express, and further secured by tapes stretched across.

Any hats having trimmings tempting to moths must have bits of camphor wrapped in tissue paper tucked about.

Untrimmed hats can be put away in groups of a kind or price, with tissue paper between, and should be stood on end, with long slips of paper clipped over the edge of each box or pasted on the wrapping paper, telling just what the parcel contains, and this placed conspicuously outward, so that any article may be quickly found.

Frames should not be put away, but *used up,* as even

in winter many wire frames are needed; but if buckram frames are left over, as these are of no use in summer, pack them away carefully, and every one can be used by making slight changes later on.

Look over the trimmed stock, and have all nicely freshened; if necessary, have the bows taken off, ripped, brushed, rubbed with a pad of clean muslin, and if necessary "steamed," then remade and replaced.

Go over all flowers, straighten out petals and leaves, and make the article look as if it had but just come from the workroom.

So many pretty and effective things can be made by steaming creased ribbons and bits of lace and combining them, draping the lace over slightly soiled parts of the ribbon, or veiling a silk drapery with a bit of net, tulle or chiffon.

Renovating Hats

The brims of leghorns can be changed from flats to mushroom or saucer brims. By immersing in water the edge contracts, and can then be molded by the fingers or over a buckram frame to the desired shape, pressing the inside of the brim with a hot iron over a cloth, and the inside of the crowns with a very small round iron.

Panama hats can be done in the same way.

Straw hats that have become discolored can be tinted to a darker shade with one of the several good colorings advertised.

To clean leghorns, panamas, milans and other fine straws, make a solution of oxalic acid and hot water, one teaspoonful to the pint, and brush thoroughly with a long-handled nail brush, taking care that the acid does not touch the hands; rinse immediately in clear hot, then cold, water; wipe off as much moisture as possible, then pin a bit of rag to the brim and thereby pin it up to dry in the air or heat; when partly dry press into shape with a hot (but not scorching) iron with muslin over the straw, on the wrong side.

When oxalic acid is not to be had, or is not necessary,

scrub well with Hand Sapolio, and rinse in several clear waters, then dry and treat as before directed.

Black straw hats may be freshened by brushing over with a mixture of good black ink and gum Arabic—after thoroughly brushing and cleaning—or if only a slight new gloss is wanted, brush over with white of egg.

Delicate silk braids must be cleaned in gasoline. Hair and tuscan braids can be cleaned with ivory soap and water only, and stains taken out with oxalic acid.

If a bowl or mushroom is desired, the hat must be held up and a bit of the brim pressed at a time till all is

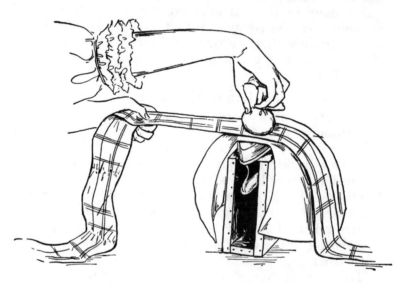

FIG. 4—STEAMING RIBBON
RUBBING OUT CREASES WITH WAD

done; in a bowl shape the movement is sideways from the crown outward (Fig. 7), but a flat or bell brim is pressed with point of iron toward the crown (Fig. 6).

If a flat brim is desired, press flat on the *table edge*, allowing the crown to come *below* the table top; afterward lay flat, with crown up, and put heavy weights around the edge of brim till perfectly dry (Fig. 6).

White and light felts and beavers are cleaned with white cornmeal, just as one cleans light furs, but shiny, greasy dark felts may be rubbed with alcohol or ether, then finished with a bit of old dark suede.

Renovating Trimmings

Gold and silver trimmings are cleaned with alcohol, and afterward burnished with chamois.

White and light-colored ostrich feathers and aigrettes can be cleaned in gasoline, as also paradise plumes, and

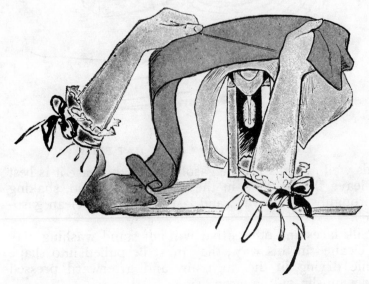

FIG. 5—STEAMING A PIECE OF BIAS VELVET (NOTE JOIN)

when clean may be given a second bath with a little tube oil color mixed in, to tint them to any desired shade; or the ends only may be tinted or shaded. Hang in the air to dry, and remember when using gasoline to have no lighted fire or gas anywhere near. When perfectly dry they can be curled as desired.

If white feathers are very dirty, ivory soap should be shredded and dissolved in a little hot water and the

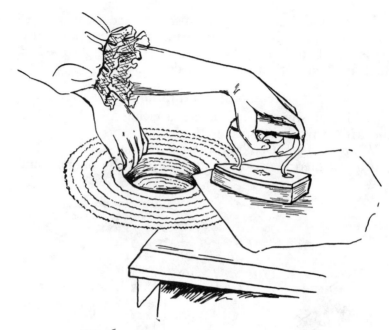

FIG. 6—PRESSING A FLAT HAT BRIM

suds well mixed with the gasoline. In this case it is best
to leave the feathers in the bath a day or so, shaking
thoroughly at intervals, and lastly rinsing in clean gasoline.

Silk laces and others that will not stand washing may
be cleaned in this way; they must be pulled into shape
while drying in the open air, and afterward pressed
under muslin on the wrong side.

Washable laces are put in a good suds of ivory soap
in a glass jar and shaken frequently, changing the water
several times; finally rinse, and pin out carefully, right
side up, on a very thickly covered board; when nearly
dry unpin and turn and press out the design with
the round end of an orange stick or ivory penholder
(Fig. 8).

If the lace needs a little stiffening, dissolve a little
gum Arabic and mix with the rinsing water. If desired

222

ecru, rinse in tea or coffee, according to the shade wanted, and in saffron tea for lemon shade. For other shades and colors Diamond dyes are best.

Steaming Velvets and Ribbons

The "steaming box" is an indispensable accessory in every workroom. Get from the grocer a small strong

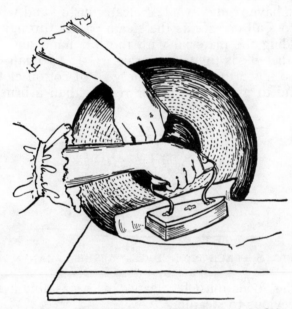

FIG. 7—PRESSING A CURVED HAT BRIM

box, and at the hardware store enough very thin sheet tin or iron to cover the top.

Have some one saw a piece out of one side as shown in Fig. 1; place the tin over the top, turn the edges over and nail down around the sides; cut a slit in the tin at the opening, bend the edges down, and nail to the sides of the opening with short, strong tacks. The slit in the box should be 3 inches wide at its open end, running to 1 inch at its inner end, and it should be not more than 8 inches long; if longer, the iron would fall through.

223

When the iron is hot take it up with the iron holder, with the point away from you; stand the wide end on the box over the narrowest end of the slit (Fig. 2), and lower the handle down into the slit. Now you are ready to steam your goods (Fig. 3).

Over the iron lay a wet clean white muslin rag, and on this hold the material to be renovated; if silks or ribbons, have ready a wad of clean muslin and with this rub across all creases as the steam passes through (Fig. 5), holding the material with the left hand and brushing so the silk is tight and straight. If two can do the work, so much the better. The wad of cotton cloth will be found to give much better results than a brush. If

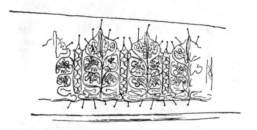

FIG. 8—LACE PINNED OUT AFTER CLEANING

dirty, the goods must be cleaned with gasoline a day at least previous to steaming.

Velvet is steamed over the wet cloth, holding it as much as possible on the straight, with, of course, the back of the goods on the cloth, and *never brush the surface* (Fig. 4). If so badly creased that this cannot be removed, it can be improved by "mirroring" it after the steaming. To do this lay it flat and pass the iron over the face of the velvet the way the nap runs.

Once having started the pass of the iron, do not stop till the end is reached, as every stop will show, and when taking the second pass let it overlap the first a little, so no unmirrored places may be left. This is done right on the velvet, no cloth between. Ribbon velvet is done in the same way, and plush becomes handsomer by this treatment. If dirty, clean first in gasoline.

Tulle and chiffon can be steamed out by holding it opened out close over, but not on, the cloth-covered iron, but flattened nozzles are sold to put on a tea-kettle spout, which when boiling projects a fan of condensed steam, very useful in renovating fragile fabrics.

If dirty, clean first in gasoline.

Wings, birds and breasts can be cleaned with corn-meal, but must be very carefully handled or the feathers will clog; gasoline is good in some cases, but, as this will dissolve glue, very few "made" pieces can be treated this way.

N. B.—The steaming box shown in Figs. 4 and 5 is made of four pieces of wood 1 inch thick nailed together. In this box the inside of slot is entirely lined with zinc, this being adjusted before the pieces are joined. The two sides measure 8 inches long by 4½ deep; the bottom is 8 by 4; the back, fitted in, 4 by 2.

LESSON XV

STARTING A MILLINERY BUSINESS

WHEN one searches for the cause of individual failures it may usually be traced to ignorance of the business and its needs; a competent milliner, in a carefully selected location, who is a judicious manager, has ninety-nine chances in one hundred for success.

There are, however, many women who, compelled by adverse circumstances to earn their own (and often dependents') living, select the millinery business because it is attractive and "looks easy." Such a woman, who has possibly never even trimmed her own hat, nor had any business experience, is more than likely to lose the money she invests, unless she has the sense to learn the business first, and also gain the necessary experience in some well-conducted showroom. A year spent in this preparation will open her eyes to very much that she had not the least idea of.

A woman desiring to start a business will do well to consult the salesmen and heads of firms of reliable wholesale houses; these men are in a position to know where such a business as any particular milliner desires to open might be profitably placed, and after consulting with a number the list may be carefully considered, a few selections made, the localities visited, inquiries made as to desirable quarters, rent, facilities, etc., and the resulting information again carefully considered, and a final selection made.

There are many grades of business, but two distinct *types* only, *i. e.,* "parlor millinery" and "store millinery."

Parlor Millinery

A store may be large or small; for the cheapest to the finest trade; but a "parlor" trade means a quiet, *private* trade, which is not dependent on "window" or "transient" customers. This class of trade requires far less capital, and can be well carried on in home rooms, though some parlor millinery rooms are quite as elaborate as any store, and cater to an exclusive clientele who prefer privacy. It is, of course, a great help if the parlor has one or two windows on the street where a hat or two can be displayed.

The windows must be daintily curtained, and if on the sunny side, provided with awnings. The room should be simply but tastefully furnished; no bright colors or glaring contrasts, even if you must repaper and paint it yourself; you cannot have too many mirrors, and certainly one or two long ones, where the entire figure can be seen. Near each mirror have a small table with a hand mirror, pin cushion, hat and short pins, and a tray with hairpins of all sizes. A couple of easy chairs and several light reception chairs; this, with soft green or gray walls, and a floor covering to match—"filling" will do—with a few nice, good rugs of rich, dark colors, makes an attractive room. The furniture may be of any preferred wood, but dark woods look best, although quite cheap chairs and tables nicely enameled white are in very good taste. A few well-selected subjects in *simple* gold, black or white frames may decorate the walls, but any personal picture should be avoided. At the end farthest from the window place a large rack, painted or stained to match the furniture; on this keep your hats, each in its own box; or have a large enclosed wardrobe (with mirror front if possible). Have this fitted with shelves, line with paper, and on these shelves lay your stock. A large chiffonier is also a most useful piece in which to keep your unmade stock. If racks are used, curtains on rings running on a brass rod should be hung over them, the curtains matching the walls. A similar curtain may cover a doorway leading into another room.

For an inexpensive material nothing answers better than denim, which comes now in all colors, and looks

227

extremely well. For a heavier material rep is the most useful; this comes in single and double widths, which is handy, as the racks are best hung with two curtains while one wide one is best for a portière.

It is well to remember that the carpets and rugs must be kept very free from dust, as this would soon destroy your stock; newspapers torn into strips and well dampened, scattered over the carpet, will prevent the dust rising when sweeping, and a few drops of ammonia in the water will keep the carpet fresh looking.

For the milliner who cannot afford made boxes, there are folding boxes. These are not only much cheaper but take up very little space, being kept flat until needed, when they are quickly formed into box shape.

Made boxes come in "nests"; that is, you can have three or four sizes, each set fitting inside the largest one, so that nine or twelve take up only the space of three; this is an object where space is limited.

Be generous in lighting; if you can get electric light, so much the better; if not, use the best gas lighting obtainable. If you are in a country place where lamps are the only light, get the best, and have an *even all over* arrangement.

Do not have your work table in full sight of your customers (supposing your one room must be show and work room combined); set a screen around it, or even curtain it off; there will be many little things you will have to do that it is not well to have customers see. Also, if you have help, it is best to keep them invisible, unless wanted outside; of course, a workroom separate from the parlor is much the best.

The Store

In opening a store very much more is required; just how much, depends on the grade of trade, but simplicity is indispensable. The entire decorations must harmonize; it may be white and gold, or black and gold, or soft reseda green with lines of palest green and gold, or two grays with silver. With white all the furniture should be the same; with black, "mission" style can be used, or dull black stain on a lighter make of furniture; with green and gray, cherry or mahogany look best; and all this can be done cheaply or very well, the latter, of course, being the most lasting, and therefore cheapest in the end.

For a good or even medium trade a large window is not necessary, but small or large, it must be enclosed with sliding glass doors or sashes, and daintily curtained.

In a cheap trade, which is more a "window" or "transient" trade, it should be large, and as it must always show a good stock, the necessity of *dust-proof* sliding glass doors will be seen.

Most millinery stores catering to medium and cheap trade do also a counter trade in trimmings; this counter must harmonize with the rest of the fittings and have a good glass counter case set on top, with a tall case at one end for some special piece of millinery and any little extra choice trimmings. Such counters and cases can be purchased second-hand, and decorated to match the general scheme.

For the rest, the portion of the store set apart for trying on may be treated similarly to the "parlor," though in a high-priced trade divisions formed by screens, each containing a long mirror, chair, and little table, will be necessary, as many women insist on privacy in being fitted to hats, as much as if they were being fitted with gowns.

In elaborate establishments the screened partitions are developed into delightful little arbors, or boudoirs, of mirror, gilding and lace.

Nowadays, when the evening or restaurant hat is made a special feature, a dark room with brilliant electric light is necessary to test colors and effects of becomingness for the chapeau as well as the robe.

The better the trade, the less stock should be on view, but racks, cases, and drawers fitted around the walls, to hold the hats, arranged according to price, style, etc., so that anything wanted can be found at once without trouble.

Waiting on Customers

The right position to try on a hat or bonnet is to stand behind the customer sitting facing the mirror. The light falling on the face should be good, but soft; a glare is unbecoming, and bad light makes shadows which are always fatal to good effects.

As the hat is set on the head, the competent saleswoman (and milliner) knows in an instant if it will fit, or suit the lines of the face; a little pull or bend often gives the right touch, but if that is not feasible, remove the hat quickly and substitute another. The saleswoman must show a real interest and personal care in her customer's appearance, and convince her that she does not want her to buy any but the right thing.

A saleswoman who is also a milliner has a great advantage, as she can design for her customers more intelligently; but unless a milliner does her own selling, this is not often the case. For this reason there is a distinct gain in the partnership of a good milliner and a saleswoman, the two working together very nicely.

Remember that your *customers work for you.* Every successful chapeau that goes out will bring more business, but in entering a new field it takes time to learn your trade; for this reason it is best to begin modestly and branch out a little each season as your trade increases.

Delivering Goods

Be very careful to nicely box each purchase; plenty of white tissue paper, which can be got very cheaply, and *care in packing,* will show your customers that you think well of your work, and the world values you as you value yourself.

Dress in the Showroom

Study your own appearance; be tastefully but *simply*

dressed, and above all let your hair be arranged in the most up-to-date style that is becoming to you. Bright colors should not be allowed in a saleswoman's dress any more than in the furniture; black or neutral tones, with white shirtwaists, are correct. The saleswoman's appearance does much toward setting off and selling her hats.

Taking Orders

In taking orders from new customers, unless they are well and satisfactorily known to you, it is customary to politely ask a deposit. One must remember that there are unscrupulous women who will take up the time of a saleswoman, trying on many hats, even leaving orders, without the slightest intention of buying. In the high-priced establishments great care is exercised that undesirable persons shall not be waited on. Saleswomen soon learn to know this type of "shopper," and politely *bow them out.*

Never let customers think you are not busy. The more people think you have to do, the more trade they will bring you.

Make light of alterations, no matter if it means re-making the entire hat—unless it is to please a customer when the hat has been *made to her order.*

In taking an order, make your calculation carefully; remember that a price once made must be adhered to, even though it entails loss, and endeavor never to disappoint in delivery if promised at a certain time. Also, it is wisest to have the customer come in to try on the finished chapeau; if sent home, it's ten chances in eleven that it will come back, whereas if you put it on her, a nip here or there will give it the right touch that makes it perfect. Never show an incomplete or half-finished order.

Buying

Unless you can give excellent bank and other references, it is wisest to pay cash for the first two seasons; then, when the houses you deal with know you, know that you are doing a steadily improving trade, they will gladly allow you the monthly credit. You are the gainer by paying cash, as, of course, the discount is better, and if you do a cash trade, is by far the best and cheapest method. But in a credit trade one is often hampered for ready money, and many a milliner finds it all she can do, even in a prosperous season, to meet the monthly bills, because her *wealthy* clientele have not paid their bills.

Salesmen are a most persuasive set, but you must know your requirements and not order anything but what you know you can sell. It is so easy to run up a long bill before you realize it; get *necessaries* first, then as much variety in the stock as you can afford, but of novelties only a sprinkling; such things as are dependent on the fashion of the moment must be very carefully considered from the standpoint of the trade you cater to.

We have in a previous lesson treated of the care of stock; it is therefore unnecessary to go into detail here, only to add that a conscientious salesman who knows the neighborhood of your location can and will help you select the right stock to start with.

Some people think it shows importance to snub the "drummers." This is a great mistake; in the first place, it is very ill bred; in the second, it is poor policy, as the drummer can help you very much. Courtesy costs nothing, and is a good investment.

Never put all your capital into a first venture, be it large or small; there are always so many unlooked-for expenses that a reserve fund is an absolute necessity.

Selling Prices

The rule in the trade is to charge double the *cost* of the hat; but, as a fact, the high-priced milliners get much more than this ratio. They have to, as their seasons are so short, their expenses tremendous, and their loss on left-overs proportionately large.

In the cheap cash trade, on the other hand, $1.00 is all

the profit made on a hat selling at from $4.00 to $6.00, while 50 cents represents the margin on a hat marked $3.50 or less, and it is only by selling a quantity that such a trade shows good profits.

Experience proves that a medium-class trade is safest and in the long run pays best. The profits are moderate, but the returns are, as a rule, cash, and enable the shrewd buyer to pick up good bargains when offered. A careful buyer will never have a bad stock on her shelves, and she will know how to turn all she buys to good profit.

Partnership

As mentioned above, a combination of the talents of a good saleswoman and a milliner should prove a most judicious and profitable one, if the trade is large enough to afford a good living for two. It happens that a pleasing saleswoman has a following good enough to warrant her starting for herself; in such case she will be distinctly the gainer by accepting a good milliner as partner, rather than pay her a salary, as she will naturally secure her fullest interest.

Many a milliner beginning business has had to do her work at night, the days being taken up in seeing customers; this is "burning the candle at both ends," and must result in disaster; it would be better to take a saleswoman, who can also help in the work, as partner, even if the returns for both are less at first.

Help

Now that so much can be got "ready-to-wear" and "ready-to-trim," and well-made, stylish hats at as little as you can make them for, the start in business is made easy for the milliner; she can get her "opening" all ready-made, and need hire no help till she sees the need of it. What kind of help she hires depends first on her own ability; if she is a trimmer, she will need a "maker," whom she pays from $5.00 to $10.00 a week; and she should also hire a girl as apprentice, paying her a little, with the understanding that she sweeps and dusts the show and work room, takes home orders, and goes shopping. Such a girl should, however, not be required to do anything outside of the business, and be conscientiously taught the trade, and retained during the dull season, when she can be kept busy making all sorts of little odds and ends for use and sale when the busy time comes.

The trimmer or maker, however, is engaged for the "season" only, this period varying, according to place and trade, from 10 to 20 weeks. A trimmer's salary runs from $10 up, many receiving $40 and over a week. Salaries must be paid weekly, the hours of work being usually from 8 A. M. to 6 P. M., with an hour for lunch. If there is a rush, the help will be expected to stay one or two evenings a week, but not the apprentices.

Where several trimmers are employed there is always one who has charge of the room, takes charge of stock needed for making up, keeps lists of what is used, and otherwise oversees matters in the workroom to see there is no waste of either time or material.

A trimmer with two makers and apprentices should turn out at least six hats a day, and many times more if they are mostly trimmings.

In hiring help from a distance, as, for instance, having a wholesale house send a trimmer or maker from New York to some distance, the employer pays the fare; if she remains the season her fare back is also paid, but if not found satisfactory within two weeks she pays her own fare to wherever she wishes to go.

Keeping Accounts

So necessary is it that every woman starting in business should be able to keep accounts systematically that bookkeeping should be learned.

Even in the most modest venture it will be found necessary to keep strict account of goods bought, used, and sold; and a "set" of books can be bought, and a small book of instructions which will give the beginner the help she needs; the set should include an "order" book and a "stock" book in which every item used for orders, or stock hats, is to be entered.

A weekly balancing of accounts will keep the proprietress informed of just how she stands.

Sketching hats from models is also a most useful accomplishment.

The Workroom

Every workroom, be it attached to a store, parlor, showroom or screened place, should have a good light; one cannot expect good work done in poor light, either daylight or artificial. Good ventilation and warmth in winter should also be assured those who have to spend their days there. Consideration for health and comfort is what every employer owes to his help, who surely will repay such care with better service.

The table should be so placed that the light falls *along* it, so that all may get their share. Chairs should be cane seated, with *flat,* not round, wood backs, and a little wooden footstool provided for each person.

A rack for boxes, in which each one can put away her work at night, and a rack with hooks for outdoor apparel are also necessary.

In another lesson we gave designs of home-made steaming boxes and their use, but there are several excellent steamers advertised for those who can afford the most up-to-date fittings for the workroom. A little stove for boiling a kettle or heating an iron is a necessary attachment, also an ironing board or table large enough to take an entire width of velvet.

LESSON XVIII

THE DESIGNER IN THE WORKROOM

A DESIGNER'S work in the millinery workroom, as in that of the modiste, is to evolve new and beautiful ideas, using the fad or fashion of the hour as a keynote, and varying its application in unlimited designs.

Most designers have some special style of chapeau in which they excel; one is more happy in her bonnets than in hats; another gives us finer designs in large hats; another seems to evolve lines of most artistic beauty in the draping of toques, etc., etc.; rarely does one find a designer who is equally excellent in every line of headwear, and it is well that it is so.

But though one may have a prolific brain, when it comes down to sifted facts we all imbibe ideas—maybe unconsciously—from outside sources; from the designs of others, from old or modern paintings and drawings, and a hundred and one various inspiring visions.

Paris is still, as it has been for many centuries, the fount of Sartorial Art. It was not always so; before the eleventh century Italy led the fashions of the then civilized world, but with the advent of the first traveling tailor and costume maker (who was a Frenchman) the tide turned, and from then on France led in the cut and make of clothing both of men and women.

It was, however, the men in those days who wore, like the birds they robbed, the gayest plumage on most picturesque hats. The headdresses of the ladies for several hundred years were disfiguring rather than enhancing to the wearer; but by degrees the hideous caps and horns disappeared, women showed more of their hair, and its dressing and decoration became an art, leading in time to the other extreme, when the structures of hair and the added trimming, such as feathers. bows, flowers,

236

baskets of fruit and flowers, and even ships in full sailing rig, rose to such proportions that the roofs of the sedan chairs of that period had to be taken off to permit of the ladies sitting inside.

But Art is a goddess that will not be denied, and soon her sway caused saner and more beautiful ideas to prevail, and from the time of Louis XVI Parisian designers have been the arbiters of fashion for the world we call civilized.

Women's chapeaux were at first the work of men, the name of milliner being a modernization of "milaner," as a native of Milan, Italy, was the first to travel in this capacity, and Milan hats are to this day highly esteemed.

After a time the clever French women took most of this trade out of the hands of the men, and with the exception of a few notable "men milliners," have held the prerogative ever since.

Paris has, however, long since ceased to be the only place where one finds really artistic designers. True, she still leads in dictating the season's modes, but she is willing, and even anxious, to accept the suggestions and follow the ideas of her American customers, for it has come to pass that the American woman has "grown up," and has come into her *heritage* of artistic ideas, and every refinement that culture and ancestry can yield her.

Artistic taste is due to temperament, and where this exists the simplest materials lend themselves to artistic combinations and beautiful effects.

The French excel in dainty, graceful designs because of their volatile, mirth-loving temperaments; the Germans can never reach these heights, because their temperaments are just the reverse, while it has been proved in several workrooms that next to the French the Irish temperament is the most artistic.

The more artistic the general training of a person, the more ready are they to appreciate and profit by the fine productions of others; hence we are glad to see and grateful for the privilege of studying the "models" brought from Paris each season by the enterprising importers.

Twenty-five years ago in Paris and London the houses that catered to America and the Colonies put aside for this trade any designs that were too extreme or "screaming" for the fastidious home buyers; but times have changed, and the American woman is now considered the best dressed in the world, and the leaders of American society are the women who dictate, quite as much as the *élite* of France.

We must concede their full merit to the Parisian designers, and those milliners who are sent over by their employers from season to season have an inestimable advantage which should bring great good to the workrooms they are connected with; the influence of such an education should be felt by the least little apprentice in the place, that every small detail of work may be the better for the investment of capital and the artistic experience of the head of the department.

In saying this we cast no reflections on the home designer; each workroom has its own class of customers to please, and each can adopt and adapt just as much of the Parisian ideas shown as suits their especial trade. Often the home design is an improvement on the model —judged from the standpoint of individual needs.

A great many "Openings" show hats marked with the tag of a Parisian firm which never saw Paris; some, if truthfully offered as "Designed in our own workrooms," would reflect great credit on the house; others are libels on any firm whose name they "borrow"; and few are so made as to deceive the knowing ones.

It is a fact, however, that the first pattern hats of the season, put on the market weeks before the first case arrives from Paris, are, as a rule, more practical and better sellers than those later evolved after the imported ideas; the home designers evidently know best what the bulk of the home market needs.

But the retail milliners, and especially those that cater

to an exclusive and private trade, find their success in being able to create designs for the *individual*. The hat *must be becoming;* it must have just enough of the prevailing mode to be up-to-date, but its finest artistic touch must be its individual tone as being a part of the wearer's personality.

Paris models cost in Paris from one hundred to one thousand francs; to this add 60 per cent. of duty, besides freight, packing, and the expenses of the buyer, and the cost is easily doubled. Yet the wholesale importers often sell such hats for less than they cost them in Paris, for the simple reason that they make their profit on the materials milliners buy to reproduce the models, these copies ranging from about half to one-fifth the cost of the originals, besides the many detail ideas that can be employed in other designs, at very considerably lower prices.

It is amazing the really artistic designs in fairly good materials that are produced by manufacturers, and also retail milliners making a specialty of low-priced hats.

Simplicity is the keynote of true art; it is not the quality of materials nor great quantities of trimming that count, but graceful lines and a *harmony of values* in the design. One simple idea, correctly carried out, is far more effective than a mixture without any special *motif.*

The Parisian designers use, as a rule, simple shapes; to these they give the lines their inspiration dictates; then the shape makers copy those lines, and "new" frames are produced.

But there are other creations that do not depend on any shape, such as a piece of velvet or felt draped over a frame, or on a hat; such designs are hard to copy; no two pairs of hands drape a given piece of material just the same way, and often in a model the piece used is simply a queer cutting left over from some garment, which makes it impossible to copy. Actually, the only and right thing to do is to take the idea and supplement

239

it with one's own artistic ability to produce a *similar* effect.

The study of paintings and good illustrations in art galleries is an excellent and most delightful method of inspiration for the designer, especially when fashion favors some special "period" of a by-gone age. There are the several "Louis" periods, the "Directoire," Empire, 1830, 1850, etc.; and we do occasionally revert to even earlier times, and adapt to modern ideas some pretty effect used by the belles of ancient times.

LESSON XIX.

The Making and Use of the Bandeau.

THE bandeau has become so much a part of millinery methods for attaining certain poise and effect, that its use and usefulness must be carefully considered.

Bandeaux range from a small form added under-

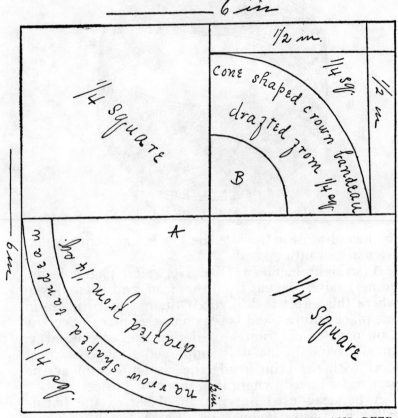

FIG. 10.—SHOWING HOW TO DRAFT SHALLOW AND DEEP BANDEAUX FROM QUARTER SQUARE.

neath (See No. 1 on page of diagrams) to some part of a hat to carry a bit of trimming; to an all round form as large as the crown of a hat; which is used either as a crown under a plateau, or to set inside a very soft crown of felt or braid.

The forms of bandeaux are as various as their use; a very much curved bandeau (See No. 2 on page of diagrams) sets down on the head, and is chiefly used when the head size is very small, the upper line fitting

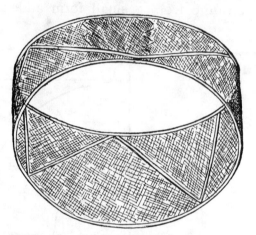

FIG. 11.—BANDEAU OF CAPE NET.

the head line of hat, while the lower line being wider, gives a well fitting band.

A straight bandeau (See No. 3 on page of diagrams) raises the hat from the head, and is employed where this effect is desired; if the hat is to tilt up in one place only, a band is set on at this place (See No. 4 on page of diagrams) or if the head size is large, an all round bandeau is employed dropped almost level with the brim inside the crown, except at the part to be raised, where it is made to project.

A bandeau used only at the back of the hat is called a "Cache Peigne" or "Catch Comb." These are used when fashion dictates the turning up of brims at the back, when the bandeau not only serves to hold the hat brim on the head, but carries a trimming which invariably accompanies this style of hat. (See Nos. 7 and 8 on page of diagrams.) No. 8 shows a curved "Cache Peigne." This is employed when the hair is dressed very full at the back, the curve allowing it to spring out over the hair puffs. The curve in the middle of No. 7 (Page of diagram) is intended to fit above the coiffure, with the trimming fuller on either side.

Of course the style of hair dressing in vogue at any given time, has a great deal to do with the shape of bandeaux most useful to give hats their right pose on this coiffure; it is therefore impossible to say what particular shape or size of bandeau is to be used on any shape hat; a half dozen different bands will give as many different effects to the same shape of hat, but the lines bent in the hat, and the pose of the trimming dictate and govern the size and shape of the bandeau.

In No. 9 (Page of diagrams) we have a side bandeau which gives a peculiar tilt, gradually raising the left side of hat, to quite a deep angle near the back; something on the order of the Gainsboro tilt.

As suggested in the lesson on frame making, the shaped bandeau can be draughted from the square (Fig. 10a) adding to this for deeper parts, or shaving off if necessary. The shallower the slope, i. e., the larger the square from which the section is cut; and if the top of a deep bandeau is to be much smaller than the base, it can be cut from a smaller square (Fig. 10b). Such bandeaux are also called crown bandeaux, and used as crowns, they may be deep or narrow as required.

Bandeaux can be made of buckram, Esparta or sheet willow, cape net, or entirely of wire like wire frames. If of buckram or willow they need only the two edge wires, if of cape net they need "bracing"

(Fig. 11); such bandeaux are used for hats of delicate materials such as tulle, etc., and need not be covered with velvet or silk; they are usually bound with narrow ribbon or velvet, and covered with the material of which the hat is made. At the same time one finds them covered with silk or velvet on the best Parisian hats, as these are usually made over cape net frames, rarely over buckram or willow.

The wire bandeau is more often the accompaniment of a wire frame; it can be covered as needed, either the material of which the hat is made, as in the case of a shirred effect, when the bandeau is similarly

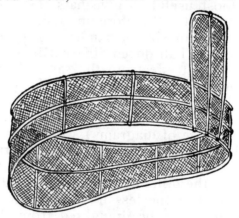

FIG. 13.—BANDEAU TO SET IN TURBAN

treated, or it is covered plain with a thin inexpensive material and the better material draped over this; there can be no rule for this, it entirely depends on the needs of the special model. Quite often the bandeau is covered with straw braid to match the hat.

Sometimes if a headsize is much too large, it is necessary to set a shaped bandeau inside the crown, the upper line touching the sides of crown but the lower line being as much less in circumference as is necessary to fit the wearer's head, for this one use Fig. 10a with the narrower circumference downward.

244

In the same way if the headsize is too small, the same bandeau is used, with the smaller circumference just outside the head line, and the wider line brought out to fit the head; if desired deeper at any given point, this depth is added and graduated off.

The more curve you give your bandeau, the more spring there is, and therefore less elevation; the straighter your bandeau, the more it will raise the hat from the head.

No. 4 is used in front when a decided front lift is wanted, as in children's Directoire bonnets, in hats of this order it is cut longer, running more around the sides. It is also used in women's bonnets where the

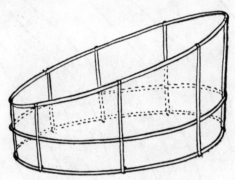

FIG. 12.—WIRE BANDEAU

shallow shape is inclined to slip back from the head; and it is most useful to give a toque a slight tilt, where a smart touch is desired; being made long or short, narrow or wide as the design, shape or wearer may need.

The use of the crown bandeau is manifold. When used as a support in soft felt, Neapolitan or other soft braid hats, it is frequently necessary to make it with "braces" attached, which extend in pear shaped loops across the brim of the hat; these have to be buttonhole sewn on as directed in Lesson VI, Fig. 9, for Leghorn or chip: but this is only when no part of the bandeau is to come below the head line; if the bandeau is intended to raise the hat, as well as support the crown, the braces must be put on the brim

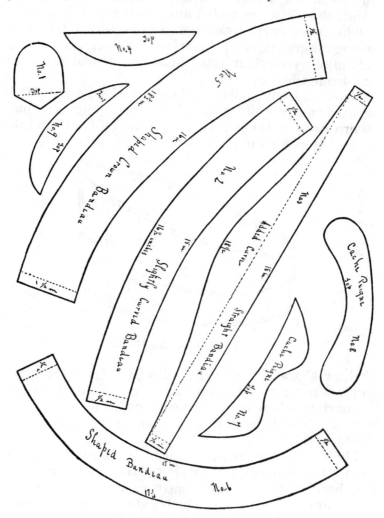

first, the ends of wires turned up inside the crown, and the bandeau put in after.

It is an open question if bandeaux should be put in

before or after the head lining of a hat; we will say to this that as the bandeau is in most cases an accessory to make the hat fit in a certain pose, it should be put in last, because no two women wear their hair alike, and the bandeau will need adjusting to the one who buys the hat; it will therefore be far less trouble if it has been put in last.

But where the bandeau forms a part of the hat, as in the case of a crown bandeau, in a soft felt, etc., or as head piece for a plateau, naturally it is put against the hat and the lining put in after; if the coiffure or other peculiarities of the wearer necessitate a change, an *extra* bandeau must be set on.

A simple bandeau, very light, is often made of one or more rows of willow braid wired; these must be covered with velvet.

In making cape net bandeaux the wire can be buttonhole sewn on the edge, but it will be firmer and stronger if a quarter-inch margin is allowed and turned over the wire, with a run and backstitch *below* the wire.

During the dull season the apprentices should make all kinds of bandeaux. These, put in boxes according to kind and shape, will be of the greatest help, and a saving of much valuable time during the busy season.

The patterns accompanying this article are given in full (medium) size, which can be easily traced off with transparent paper and pencil, and changed to requirements, enlarging or reducing according to individual needs.

Glossary of Millinery and Dry Goods Terms.

Agrafe.—A clasp or ornament of metal for millinery purposes.

Aigrette.—A stiff plume. Sometimes erroneously applied to "egret," which see.

Ajour.—Open work effect. Also applied to a cotton braid used in the making of women's hats.

Alençon (Point d').—Fine needle-point lace with ground of double-twist thread in a semi-net effect. Usually worked with horse-hair to give firmness to the cordonnet.

Allover.—Embroideries or lace materials in which the design or pattern extends over the entire surface of the fabric in contradistinction to edges and insertions.

Amazon (Plume).—A long soft Ostrich feather.

Angleterre (Point d').—Fine Brussels pillow lace distinguished by a rib of raised and plaited threads worked in the lace.

Antique.—Imitation of silk stuffs of former centuries.

Antwerp.—Bobbin lace resembling early Alençon. Shows a "pot" or basket effect in design.

Appliqué.—Materials cut out and sewed, embroidered or pasted on other materials.

Arabian (Point d').—Coarse bobbin lace, made in Belgium, France, and Arabia. Large pattern cable edged, and almost invariably in deep ecru tone.

Argentine.—Similar to Alençon, mesh being larger.

Armure.—A chain weave in which the threads are thrown in alternating small pebbled design. Used in silks and dress goods.

Arras.—Strong, white, bobbin lace resembling Mechlin. Distinguished by light single thread ground.

Areophane.—A thin crepe like material.

Armossin.—Same as Armure.

Art Nouveau.—New Art (Ornaments).

Aurillao.—Bobbin lace which resembles Angleterre.

Ave Maria.—A narrow edging.

Baby Lace.—Light and simple edging made in England.

Bandeau.—A band or part of a band placed in the headsize of a hat to raise part or the whole of it.

Barré.—Materials having stripes or bars running across the cloth produced by various processes of weaving or printing.

Barrette.—Bar ornament for hair or headdress.

Basket Weave.—Style of weave in which the plaited work of a basket is reproduced by the pattern.

Batiste.—A fine cotton muslin having a good deal of dressing, resembling lawn, the difference being that batiste is slightly heavier.

Battenburg.—A modern lace of braid and stitches. Same as Renaissance.

Bayadère.—Designs which run across the material, whether ribbons, laces, dress goods or silks.

Bayadère Moiré.—Same as above, with watered effect.

Bayeux.—Bobbin lace in imitation of Spanish point. Also black, rich lace, made for shawls, etc.

Bébé.—Baby.—The narrowest ribbon.

Beaver.—A thick woolen cloth weave similar to doeskin. The wrong side is finished with a soft, thick nap. In hats on Plaques, a long nap fur thrown on bodies of wool and fur felt.

Bedford Cord.—A weave used in dress goods similar to cotton piqué, consisting of heavy ribs running lengthwise in the fabric. A straw braid in rough effect for making hats.

Beige.—Dress fabrics of smooth texture produced by using yarn in which the colors are mixed. Also a term applied to a color near shade of wood.

Bengaline.—A plain, round, corded weave of silk and wool in which the wool is used as a filling covered by the silk. Smooth in surface, small in grain.

Beret.—A flat cap.—(Basque Peasants). Used as crown for wide brim hats.

Bijou.—Jewel.

Binche.—Fine pillow lace, without cordonnet. Ground resembles spider web with small dots.

Bissette.—Coarse, narrow French Peasant lace, simple designs. Name applied to cheap bordering laces.

Blanche.—White.

Bluet.—Corn flower.

Blonde Lace.—Lace made of unbleached silk. Nets in cotton or silk that are unbleached or cream colored.

Bobbin Bone Point Lace.—Applied to laces having no regular ground or mesh as Renaissance.

Bobbinet or Brussels.—Machine-made cotton or silk netting in which a hexagonal figure is produced by twisting the thread.

Body Hats.—Hats of various straws pleated in one piece, shape of un-

248

finished hat or hood, also of felt, wool and beaver,

Bokhara.—A diaphanous silk of natural color in which a weave of white taffeta silk is produced.

Botany Yarn.—Yarn composed of a fine grade of Australian wool and used in the manufacture of worsted dress goods.

Bouillonné.—Narrow shirrings of chiffon that edge wide ruffles or plaitings of the same or other materials.

Bouclé.—Knotted and curled effects raised upon the surface of the cloth produced by the use of two-ply yarn in which one thread is wound around the other and partly drawn out so as to produce a loop. Rarely used in silk fabrics.

Bourbon.—A machine-made lace of both silk and cotton. Scroll-like patterns, cable edged on regular mesh.

Bourette.—An effect produced by introducing lumpy, knotted yarn in the weaving. The yarn so introduced is woven in at intervals, forming patterns or creating an evenly arranged rough surface.

Box Plait.—A double fold or plait formed by folding the cloth alternately in opposite directions so as to form a plait from each side.

Brandenburg.—A military ornament of braid and loops with which a jacket is fastened. Sometimes used on hats.

Bretonne.—Cheap narrow edging.

Brides.—Slender threads connecting different parts of pattern lace.

Bride Lace.—Laces with pattern connected with brides (meaning bridges.) Same as bone point lace.

Brilliant.—Indicates a finish of great luster.

Brocade.—Heavy-weight silk with raised figures of flowers, foliage, or other, sometimes gold or silver threads woven in. Any fabric with a Jacquard effect.

Brocatelle.—A damask, principal figures having raised surface.

Broché.—An effect where the warp design is raised in floats and appears as though embossed on the surface of the fabric.

Brodé.—Embroidered effects either on silks, woolens or cottons.

Brussels Net.—Plain net made originally in Brussels, but now made in all lace countries.

Brussels Pillow.—Fine pillow lace with patterns joined together by little loops on their edges.

Brussels Point.—Shows open pattern made in partly open and partly closed stitch, giving appearance of shading.

Buckram.—Cotton cloth two or more ply united and stiffened with Agglutenates.

Butcher's Linen.—A plain weave fabric of linen used for dress purposes, similar to crash in appearance but lighter in weight and composed of smoother yarns.

Cabochon.—A round buckle or brooch.

Cachepeigne.—Literally "hide comb." Any trimming on a hat that fulfils this purpose, but more correctly the trimming should be placed beneath the back rim.

Camel's Hair.—A loosely woven woolen fabric in which a very long fiber is employed. It is composed of the finest worsted.

Canile.—A jointed effect with stripes broken at intervals by knots or small squares.

Cannelé.—A channel effect in weaving giving lengthwise stripes in raised or lowered effect on the goods in small patterns.

Canotier.—Sailor style, cloth or hat.

Canton.—A cheap chine straw braid.

Capeline.—Hat with soft brim.

Cape Net.—Stiff finished Nottingham net. Sometimes called rice net.

Capote.—Close hat toque or cap.

Capuchon.—A hood for evening wear.

Carreau.—A square check.

Carrickmacross.—Tiny Irish cambric drawn-work appliqué on net.

Cartisane.—Guipure or passementerie, made on thin silk or gilt covered strips of parchment.

Cashmere.—A wool fabric twilled on one side only, with soft finish.

Challie.—An extremely light-weight dress fabric, cotton or wool, woven without twill, free from dressing.

Chameleon.—A three-toned glacé effect.

Champagne.—Delicate golden ecru.

Changeant.—Changeable effects in color produced by crossing the weaves.

Changeant.—Changeable. Iridescent.

Chantilly.—Pillow lace very similar to blonde. Made in both silk and cotton.

Chapeau.—Sing. Chapeaux, plu. (hat) (hats).

Cheesecloth.—Thin muslin, bleached or brown, free from sizing.

Cheviot.—Twilled, nappy woolen cloth.

Chic.—Pronounced "shik." Smart. Good style.

Chiffon.—A transparent fine woven silk gauze.

Chiffonette.—The flimsiest and most bodiless of the chiffon family.

Chiffon Taffeta.—An exceedingly thin light-weight taffeta.

Chiffon-Velours.—The lightest and softest velvet known.

Chiné.—Fabrics in which the pattern is printed on the warp, so that when woven the crossing threads show the design in a broken effect, giving the appearance of shadows, etc.

Chip Braid.—An Italian and Japanese woodchip plait, used in the making of women's hats.

Chou.—(Choux.) A large rosette of ribbon, silk or tulle.

Ciel.—Sky blue.

Cluny.—Coarse thread bobbin lace, made in both linen and cotton. Close stitch pattern darned on open ground.

Coque.—Cock feathers.

Coquilled.—Fanned or fluted trimming.

Coquelicot.—Brilliant poppy red.

Coquille.—Fluted or scalloped like a shell.

Cordé.—In ribbed or corded effect, woven, stitched or made, lengthwise or crosswise of the goods.

Corduroy.—A heavy ribbed cotton material made like velvet, with a twilled foundation and a pile surface.

Couteau.—A knife-like quill or wing.

Covert.—A twilled diagonal cloth usually made in mixtures for tailoring.

Craponne.—Cheap, stout thread furniture guipure.

Crêpe.—French for crape. A puckered or crinkled fabric.

Crêpela.—A small crêpe-like effect.

Crépon.—A crinkled dress fabric made of silk or wool or mixed. Also cotton.

Crêpe de Chine.—A crinkled, thin silk dress fabric.

Crêpe Lisse.—A zephyr gauze of silk plain woven.

Craquellé.—Crackled or broken glass effect in lace, net or silk.

Croisé.—A cross twill in weaving. Applied to velvets means twilled back instead of the old straight back

Crystal.—A heavy corded silk with wool filling in which the small cords alternate with large, regular or irregular cords.

Damask.—A fabric with flat figures formed by contrast between warp and filling surfaces.

Damassé.—Fabrics ornamented on the surface with a rich design, the running figure woven, but not printed—same as damask.

Damier.—A check pattern. Equivalent to checkerboard.

Darned Lace.—Comprehensive term taking in all net effects with the pattern applied in needlework, such as filet lace.

Dessous.—Below underbrim. Foundation.

Demi Plume.—Medium size or half length feather.

Deux Tones.—Two tones.

Dieppe.—A fine needle point lace resembling Valenciennes.

Dimity.—Thin white goods, plain or printed, distinguished by raised threads or cords running lengthwise.

Directoire.—In the style of the French Directory, 1793-1801.

Drap.—Cloth.

Drap d'été.—A heavy-weight material made like cashmere.

Drap de Lyons.—A rich plain French silk made on Lyons looms.

Drap de Soie.—A somewhat heavy corded weave.

Drap-Satin.—A wool material with satin-like finish.

Dresden.—A very small, unobtrusive design. The term has been adopted from Dresden china, to designate small, neat effects in printing.

Duchesse.—A satin fabric of which the back is woven in flat twills, making a smooth face, not showing the twilled effect.

Dutch Lace.—Practically a coarse Val.

'Echarpe.—Literally a scarf. Applied to the long, floating ends in a broad stole effect employed in ladies' neckwear, also draped around hats.

Ecosser.—(This means of Scotch design or shell-like.) **Escalloped Genrie.**—A style of figure and color illustrating every-day life, manners and customs.

Ecru.—Raw, unbleached silk in its natural color. Also applied to color, a light shade of dressed pine.

Egret.—The light floating feathers obtained from the heron. (See Aigrette.)

Empire.—Styles of women's dress fashionable during the reign of Napoleon I., based on the mode of dress customary in ancient Greece.

En Carreau.—A square pattern.

English Point.—See Angleterre.

Eolienne.—A sheer silk and wool fabric.

Epinglé.—A ribbed fabric, showing

moderately large and smaller ribs alternating in plain figures and colors

Escurial.—Heavy silk lace in imitation of Rose point. Pattern outlined with cable edge.

Esprit (Point d').—Dotted bobbinet with the dots either singly or in clusters.

Etamine.—A canvas weave with a wide mesh, rendering it more or less transparent; sometimes woven with a silk stripe.

Façonné.—Figured goods in which the design is raised upon the surface. Silk or wool.

Fagoting.—A criss-cross openwork stitch done in a rope silk or thread.

Faille.—Soft ribbed dress silk or ribbon with a prominent cord extending across the fabric. Not so heavy as Ottoman, twice as large as gros grain.

Faille Français.—A faille made on French looms.

Failletine.—A light and extremely soft weave of the faille order.

Failletine Moiré.—A light faille in moiré effect.

Feston.—Loop designs, shallow wide scallops.

Filet Lace.—Any lace made with a square mesh net, with pattern darned in.

Flemish Point.—Needle point lace made in Flanders.

Fleur de Soie.—"Flower of silk." Face of satin de Lyons twill with backing interlaced with what is known as the twelve-shaft satin principle.

Fleur de Velours.—Flower of velours. A fine and very superior grade of velours.

Flitter.—Spangles made of composition, light in weight.

Floconné.—A silk dress material having small flakes of white or color.

Florentine.—A gauze weave used in making artificial flowers and for general millinery purposes.

Footing.—A simple insertion of Brussels net from one to three inches in width.

Foulard.—A soft, thin, washable dress silk woven without twill. Twilled foulard, so known, is really a silk serge.

Foundation Weaves.—There are but three—plain, twill and satin.

Fourragère.—Ornaments of braid set on each side of a bodice, and connected by one or more long, drooping cords.

Galloon.—Narrow trimming of wool, silk, tinsel, cotton, etc. Also gilt or silver lace on uniforms, liveries and band caps.

Gauffré.—An effect produced by pressure or gauffrage in calendering, by which the surface of almost any fabric can be pressed into forms of relief.

Gauze.—A very fine and peculiar weave of the bunting order. A thin voile.

Gaze (Point de).—Flemish point lace resembling point d'alençon, though much softer, being without horsehair. Not used now except in the making.

Gene (Point de).—Openwork embroidery made on wool ground afterward eaten away by acid.

Genoa.—Heavy lace made on aloe fiber. See macrame.

Gimp.—See Guipure.

Glacé.—Highly glazed material, usually in silk or woolen goods, produced in weaving. Glace gloves are those finished with a polished or dressed surface.

Grammont.—White pillow lace used for shawls, etc. Black silk lace nearly resembling blonde.

Granité.—A weave in which the yarns are twisted to a sufficient extent to give a sort of roughened surface to the material.

Granité Soie.—A rich and elegant form of falconné; color whitish gray as seen in granite rock.

Grenadine.—An openwork diaphanous material of silk, wool or cotton.

Gros Grain.—A ribbed silk fabric or ribbon with heavy thread running crosswise.

Gros de Tours.—Similar to taffeta; two or more pickings being inserted in same shed instead of one, making fine ribbed surface.

Guimpe.—A front and back yoke to be worn with low-cut dress, with or without sleeves.

Guipure.—Little fancy trimming of wire cord wound with silk or cotton threads and the pattern stitched together.

Guipure d' Art.—Linen net upon which raised-on intersecting patterns are worked.

Guipure de Flandre.—Pillow lace made separate flowers, connected by bars and brides.

Habutai.—A plain-woven silk made in Japan on hand looms. Smooth and even in texture.

Hand Embroidery.—Heavy point lace with fancy floral or other figures embroidered on design.

Harlequin Checks.—A plaid effect in three or more colors.

Haute.—High, extreme.

Haute Nouveaute.—Extreme novelty.

Hollow-cut Cord.—A pile material woven with a plain surface, on which the cord finish is cut out with a knife.

Homespun.—A silk weave in imitation of Scotch or Irish woolens.

Honiton.—English bobbin lace noted for beauty of design.

Honiton Braid.—Narrow machine-made braid of ornamental, oval figures, connected by narrow bars.

Honiton Guipure.—Large flower pattern lace on very open ground, the sprays held together with brides and bars.

Illusion.—A thin and very transparent tulle. (See Tulle.)

Imitation Hair Braid.—Cotton braid made to imitate Neapolitan used in making of women's hats. Term also applied to pyroxylin braid.

Imitation Lace.—Term used to designate any machine-made lace against hand-made.

Imprime.—French for printed.

Incisé.—An effect produced by cutting out designs in a dress material and placing silk or some other fabric underneath it, the edges of the upper material being sewed down.

Incroyable.—A style of costume modeled upon the dress of the dandies of the period of the French Directorate.

Insertion.—Any narrow lace with a plain edge on either side that admits of its being inserted in a fabric.

Iridescent.—Rainbow and shot-color effects showing prismatic hues and play of color.

Irish Crochet.—Heavy hand-made lace, remarkable for the beauty and distinctness of its patterns and the startling whiteness of the linen thread used in its manufacture.

Irish Point.—Hybrid combinations of appliqué, cut-work and embroidery on net, with elaborate needle stitching.

Jaconet.—A fine muslin, heavier than cambric, free from starch or dressing, but glazed by calendering.

Jacquard.—Applied to materials woven on jacquard looms which automatically select the threads and make the designs formerly produced on hand looms only.

Jardinière.—In flower-garden designs.

Jasper.—Black warp with white filling, forming a gray.

Jupon.—A short petticoat. Applied to the new double and triple skirts. The upper skirt is the jupon.

Khaiki.—A Japanese silk, plain woven and less fine in weave than the habutai.

Knotted Lace.—Fancy weave of twisted and knotted thread in close imitation of some old hand laces.

Laine.—Wool.

Lancé.—Lance shaped splashes over a plain ground.

Lansdowne.—A silk and wool material of very light construction.

Leghorn.—Braid of Italian weave used in making women's hats.

Liberty.—Thin, satin-finished silk.

Ligne.—Lined, striped.

Lingerie.—Pronounced "Langery." Washable.

Lille.—A French lace which resembles Mechlin. Shows a very clear, light ground and is the most beautiful of all simple thread laces.

Limerick Lace.—A form of embroidery on net or muslin.

Lisse.—A sort of chiffon of the gauze order, with a crêpe twist.

Louisine.—A silk fabric of overlapping weave producing an uneven surface which resembles that of an armure in miniature.

Louis XIV., Louis XV., Regence, Directoire, Empire, etc.—Terms used to designate the styles that prevailed in certain periods of the political history of France.

Luxeine.—Laces of a stout, heavy nature.

Luxor.—A ribbed satin or silk cloth, soft and rich.

Maco.—Strictly speaking, a yarn made of Egyptian cotton, undyed; applied to yarn in the natural color. Used for the feet or parts thereof in black and colored hosiery.

Macrame.—Knotted, hand-made lace of very heavy cord. Geometrical designs principally.

Maline.—A very fine silk net of gauze-like texture.

Maltese.—Coarse, machine-made cotton lace, resembling torchon. Has no regular ground, patterns usually connected with heavy stitch work.

Marabout.—Beautiful Indian bird.

Marabou.—Soft down-like feathers.

Marron.—Chestnut brown.

Marceline.—A thin silk used for linings. Plain made, brilliant surface.

Marly.—A cotton cloth finished and stiffened like rice net.

Matelassé.—Woolen or silk cloth which has a raised pattern on the surface as if quilted or wadded.

Mat.—Dull finish.

252

Matte.—A faint dull shade of grayish green.

Mechlin.—A light pillow lace with the pattern outlined by a fine but very distinct thread or cord, pattern running to flowers, buds, etc.

Medallion.—An ornament of lace which is applied to a garment.

Medici.—A collar for cloaks and dresses, very high and stiffened, rolling outward at the top.

Mélange.—Mixtures of color applied in weaving. Also mixtures of cotton warp and wool weft. Also hand-made silk pillow lace showing a combination of Chantilly with Spanish designs.

Melton.—Stout, smooth woolen cloth used for men's clothing and ladies' coats. The nap is sheared close to the surface and is finished without pressing or glossing.

Mercerized.—A chemical process of rendering cotton threads lustrous. The thread is shortened and hardened, producing a silky effect.

Merveilleux.—A class of fine twilled-back silk satins.

Messaline.—A light-weight silk having a lustrous surface and soft sheer weave.

Mexican Drawn Work.—Little, round medallions either singly or in strips, the threads drawn to form a cartwheel.

Mignonette.—Light bobbin lace made in narrow stripes. Also soft dull green shade.

Milan Braid.—An Italian straw weave for manufacturing hats.

Miracourt.—Sprig effects of bobbin lace applied on net ground.

Miroir.—Glossy or brilliant surface produced on pile and silk fabrics by calendering.

Miroir du Nord.—Same as above with glacial effect.

Mistral.—A sheer worsted material woven from yarns twisted to give a kinky surface to the fabric.

Mitaine.—A form of sleeve in which that part below the elbow resembles a mitten.

Mohair.—A light-weight fabric having a lustrous surface composed of the wool obtained from the Angora goat. Also applied to a tape braid used in the manufacture of hats.

Moiré.—A watered effect produced on silks.

Moiré Antique.—A fabric watered in design to imitate antique effects.

Moiré à Pois.—A watered effect with small satin dots sprinkled over surface.

Moiré Française.—A moiré effect in stripes produced by use of engraved rollers.

Moiré Impérial.—Showing an indefinite watered effect covering entire surface.

Moiré Metallic.—Presenting a watered, clouded and frosted appearance.

Moiré Nacre.—Mother-of-pearl effect showing delicate tints seen in interior of sea shells.

Moiré Ocean.—Watered in a design of wavy, undulating stripes.

Moiré Poplin.—A wool-filled, corded fabric, with watered effect.

Moiré Renaissance.—A fabric watered in Renaissance design.

Moiré Scintillant.—A scintillating or lustrous watered fabric.

Moiré Supreme.—A rich satin weave watered.

Moiré Velours.—A silk fabric with a twilled face on which a watered effect has been produced.

Monotone.—One tone or color.

Monture.—Bouquet of artificial flowers.

Moreen.—Fabric of mohair or wool filling and cotton warp. Made in imitation of moiré silk.

Motif.—The unit of a design which is repeated over and over again in a lace pattern. Frequently in a large design the motif is taken out and used separately, in which case it approximates closely to a medallion.

Mousseline de Soie.—An extremely fine, soft muslin made of silk.

Nacré.—Having the appearance of mother-of-pearl.

Nanduly.—South American fiber lace made by needle in small squares, afterward joined together.

Natté.—Tressed or basket weave. A fabric constructed in loose check design in one or more colors, in a manner to give the cloth a braided appearance.

Needle Point Lace.—See point lace.

Nid d'Abeille.—Bee-hive effect.

Noeud.—Bow twist of ribbon, cords, etc.

Noué.—Tied, knotted.

Noir.—Black.

Nouvelle.—Novelty. (Mode) **New.**—The latest mode.

Nuance.—Gradation of a color.

Normandy Lace.—See Valenciennes.

Nottingham.—Term including all machine-made laces from lace district of England.

Nouveau.—French for new, novel.

Ombré.—Graduated colorings, shading from light to dark or vice versa.

Ondine.—A thick cord Bengaline, every third cord crinkled.

Onduleux.—A wavy effect.

Organdy.—A thin, light, transparent silk or cotton muslin.

Organize.—The silk fiber doubled and twisted as "thrown" into yarn for warp thread.

Oriental Lace.—An embroidery produced on schiffle machine, pattern being cut or eaten out.

Ottoman.—Fabric of coarser rib than faille, but of faille family. May be all silk, all wool or mixture.

Oxford.—Originally a wool fabric in dark gray and white mixtures (90 per cent. of the former and 10 per cent. of the latter). Of late, heavy cotton and linen fabrics have been known by this name.

Oyah Lace.—A crocheted guipure shown in ornate patterns.

Paille.—Straw.

Paillette.—A spangle or scale. Also applied to large round spots or patterns on fabrics.

Paillette de Soie.—A silk fabric spangled with jet or gelatine.

Paillon.—Large spangle.

Paletot Coat.—The distinguishing feature of this coat is the skirts, which extend ten inches or more below the waistline.

Panaché.—Plumed.

Pannoché de Coque.—Plume of cock feathers.

Paon.—Peacock.

Paradise (plume de).—Paradise plume.

Patent Milan.—A fine weave of China straw in imitation of the Italian Milan—see Union Milan.

Plume de Paon.—Peacock plume.

Passé.—Old, out of date.

Panne.—A pile fabric of the satin antique variety. Long-haired, but not so lustrous.

Papillion Taffetas.—Showing a design of different sized spots or other, or with shot ground in designs of chine, flowers figured in butterfly or other winged designs.

Paquet.—Pompon effect in artificial flowers or feathers.

Paraguay.—Drawnwork motifs in lace and embroidery.

Parisienne.—A mixed silk and wool fabric. A woman of Paris.

Passementerie.—Heavy embroideries or edgings and galloons, especially those made of rich gimps, braids, beads, silks and tinsel.

Pastel Shades.—Very light tints somewhat opaque in character.

Pastille.—A round or oval spot; also applied to trimmings which are in lozenge design.

Peau.—French for skin, hide or pelt.

Peau de Cygne.—One of the popular weaves of soft, highly finished silk, closely resembling peau de soie.

Peau de Soie.—Silk woven like gros grain, but with a rib so fine as to produce a plain-woven face. The best grades are finished alike on both sides. The effect is satiny.

Pékiné, or Pekin Stripes.—A design in stripes of alternating colors, the stripes usually being of equal width.

Pelerine.—A small cape. A term now specially applied to a form of ladies' neckwear.

Percale.—A kind of cambric closely and firmly woven, with more dressing than ordinary muslin, printed or plain.

Persian.—A thin silk fabric formerly used for linings.

Persian Effects.—Showing peculiar designs and color tones common to cashmere shawls and other Indian textile productions.

Petits Pois.—Tiny dots or specks. French for peas.

Picot.—Small loop used as an ornamental edging on ribbons or lace.

Pillow Lace (Bobbin Lace).—Made on a pillow with bobbins and pins. Machine-made imitations retain the name.

Piqué.—Cotton cloth for making summer hats.

Piquet.—A standing or ornamental trimming of various materials for women's hats.

Plaque.—A flat round or square of smaller size than a Plateau, usually of two materials pressed.

Plastron.—Part of the garment covering the breast.

Plateau.—Sing. Plateaux, plu., a flat round or square of straw, felt, fur, velvet or any other material to drape into toques or crowns of hats.

Plauen.—A term applied to German machine-made laces made at Plauen, usually the coarser embroidered effects.

Plissé.—Plaited.

Plissé Ombré.—A new armure weave in plissé effect, and ombré shading.

Plume.—A feather.

Plume d'Aigle.—Eagle's feather or quill.

Plumetis.—A fine, sheer fabric in which a design is produced by means of loose tufts or spots.

Pointillé.—Dotted with small spots or polka dots.

Point Kant.—Flemish pillow lace with a net ground, and pot design.

Point Lace.—Lace made by hand with needle and single thread. Needle point the same.

Point Plat.—Point lace without raised design.

Pompadour.—Small flowered designs printed or brocaded in bright colors.

Pompadour Gros de Tour.—A high class gros grain with fine ribbed surface in pompadour effect.

Pompadour.—Large floral design on plain ground. 18th century.

Pompon Militaire.—Military pompon.

Pongee.—Thin, soft silk fabric woven from the natural uncolored raw silk.

Pongee Imperial.—A heavy pongee silk woven with a taffeta surface.

Popeline.—A repped wool and silk material, the warp of silk.

Poplinette.—An extremely light-weight popline weave.

Postilion.—Two ends or tabs at the back of a jacket or waist.

Pouf.—A puff of material.

Poult de Soie.—A peculiarly strong and durable silk.

Princess.—A long gown made in one continuous piece fitting closely.

Punjab Silks.—Domestic imitation of Indian fabrics.

Quadrille.—Applied usually to small checks in squares. Shepherd checks.

Queen Silk.—A very soft fabric of chiffon order.

Radia.—A 44-inch silk, Lyons weave, soft and of high luster.

Radium.—A term signifying a brilliant finish, applied to silk and braids.

Ramagé.—Patterns following the lines of branches and tendrils of plants.

Rayé.—Striped.

Rayure.—French for stripe.

Recherché.—Very choice, refined.

Redingote.—A long coat.

Renaissance.—Modern lace made of narrow tape or braid formed into patterns, held together by brides, the brides forming subsidiary patterns.

Rep.—Style of weaving in which the surface has a crosswise ribbed appearance as a distinction from "cords" which extend lengthwise in the fabric.

Repousse.—Applied to design which has effect of being stamped on.

Réséda Mignonette.—A delicate soft green.

Rhadzimer.—A sort of twill.

Rhadzimer Surah.—A surah with a modified rib across surface.

Rose Point.—See Venice.

Royale.—A modification of Gros de Tours.

Satin.—A silk cloth of close texture and overshot warp with rich, glossy surface.

Satin de Chine.—A soft drapy satin with crêpe-like finish.

Satin de Laine.—Wool satin.

Satin Grec.—A twelve harness satin in which a taffeta point is added to each place of interlacing, making cloth firmer.

Satin Serge.—A satin twill.

Satin Soleil.—A fabric with satin-like surface with a cross-line appearance and pronounced sheen.

Scintillant.—Sparkling.

Seaming Lace.—Narrow openwork insertion.

Seed Effects.—Are formed by tiny dots which give appearance as if small seeds had been strewn over surface.

Serge.—French for twill.

Seville.—Variety of torchon.

Shantung.—A heavy grade of pongee silk in which the natural color of the material is preserved.

Sicilienne.—A mohair of heavy weight, either plain or with a fancy pattern.

Silkaline.—Thin mercerized cotton cloth in imitation of silk.

Soie Batiste.—Silk batiste, a diaphanous summer fabric in very small figures or plain.

Soleil.—Name for shiny materials used in millinery trade.

Souple.—A dull effect in silk dyeing.

Spanish Lace.—Convent-made, needle point lace. Cut drawnwork, needle point lace in large squares. Heavy black silk lace in floral designs.

Spanish Point.—Ancient variety of gold, silver and silk passementeries.

Sparterette.—An imitation or a substitute for sparterie, or willow squares or sheets.

Split Straw.—Whole straw. Split having a smooth surface; used in the making of hats.

Suêde.—Leather finished on the wrong or flesh side, or having the thin, glossy outer grain shaved or peeled off, leaving an undressed surface.

Surah.—A light, soft twilled silk.

Surah Ecossais Quadrille.—A surah in design and coloring of Scotch squares.

Swiss Lace.—Swiss-embroidered net in imitation of Brussels.

Swivel Effects.—Produced by use of diminutive shuttle in figure weaving, the same carrying threads of different shades, with object of obtaining special effects in flowers, foliage, etc.

Taffeta.—A silk fabric of plain weave, with warp threads much finer and more numerous than the hard-spun filling. Surface is ribbed with warp alone showing.

Taffetas Metallique.—Taffetas finished with metallic effect.

Taffetas Uni.—Plain taffetas.

Taffetas weave.—Same as plain weave or uni.

Tambour.—Variety of Limerick.

Tape Lace.—Hand-made needle lace similar to Renaissance.

Tartan.—A thin silk. A checkered pattern or plaid such as are distinctive of the Scotch clans.

Teneriffe.—A lace stitch; a form of drawn-work in which the wheel pattern predominates.

Tête de Négre.—Niggerhead.

Thread Lace.—Made of linen thread as distinguished from cotton and silk laces.

Thrown Silk.—Material that has been doubled and spun into yarns of various sizes, in preparation for the looms.

Torchon.—A coarse open bobbin lace of stout but loosely twisted thread in very simple patterns.

Tram.—Filling, weft.

Travers.—Stripes running the direction of the filling.

Tresse.—Braid.

Tuscan Braid (Lace).—Tuscan straw used in the making of women's hats.

Tulle.—Finest silk mesh net.

Tulle Coulisse.—Trimming of shirred tulle.

Tulle.—Plain fine silk net.

Tussah.—A species of rough silk obtained from wild worms that feed on oak and other leaves of the forest.

Uni.—Plain weave.

Union Milan.—See Patent Milan.

Van Dyke Points.—Applied to laces with border made in points.

Valenciennes.—Commonly called Val. Bobbin lace seen mostly in cheap insertions in form of narrow edgings.

Velour 'Epingle.—Terry pin dot velvet.

Velour Faconne.—Figured velvet.

Velour Miroir.—Miroir velvet.

Velours.—French for velvet. A pile fabric akin to plush, produced in many forms in plain and fancies.

Velours, Albigeois.—A fancy striped

velour in two or more tones, stripes running seven or eight to the inch.

Velours Antique Ecossais.—An antique-plaited effect velours.

Velours Ecossais.—A plaid velour.

Velours Ecrase.—Similar to miroir velvet.

Velours Gros Grain.—A gros grain weave with rich, soft velvet-like finish.

Velours Ottoman.—Resembling faille Français. Broader rib than Gros de Tours and heavier binder warp.

Velours Russe.—Fabric of glacé foundation with silk cords and stripes of contrasting colors.

Velours Soleil.—Velours with bright sheen imparted in finish.

Velvet.—See Velours.

Venetian.—An all-wool material of a broadcloth construction, except that the face is twilled.

Venetian Point.—Needle point lace in floral pattern with the design very close together, connected by brides ornamented with picots.

Vert.—Green.

Vigogne.—The French form of the word vicuna; applied to a soft woolen dress material.

Vigoureux.—A worsted material printed in colors, producing a mélange effect in coloring.

Voile.—Veil, veiling.

Voile.—Veiled, clouded.

Voilette.—Small veil.

Voile or Veiling.—A fabric similar to the old-fashioned nun's veiling, but made with somewhat heavier yarns.

Warp.—The longitudinal thread in a woven fabric.

Warp Effects.—Patterns which depend mainly upon the treatment of the warp.

Warp Prints.—Fabric in which the designs have been printed on the stretched warp before weaving.

Weft.—Same as filling.

Willow Plume.—Feathers of the Ostrich, the flues of which are tied or pasted together to make them longer—in imitation of the foliage of the willow tree.

Youghal.—Needle point lace of coarse thread made exclusively in Ireland.

Ypres.—Bobbin lace somewhat coarser than Val.

Zibeline.—A dress material which to a greater or less extent imitates the fur of an animal; often the hairy effect is lessened by shearing the surface.

Titles published by R.L.Shep

ART IN DRESS (1922) by P. Clement Brown

CIVIL WAR COOKING: The Housekeeper's Encyclopedia (1861) by Mrs. E. F. Haskell

CIVIL WAR ERA ETIQUETTE: Martine's Handbook & Vulgarisms in Conversation

CIVIL WAR GENTLEMEN: Apparel Arts & Uniform

CIVIL WAR LADIES: Fashions & Needle-Arts of the Early 1860s

CLEANING, REPAIRING & CARING FOR BOOKS: A Practical Manual by R. L. Shep

COMPLETE GUIDE TO PRACTICAL CUTTING (1853) by Edward Minister & Sons

CORSETS: A Visual History (mid 1800s - 1930s)

EARLY VICTORIAN MEN (1838)

EDWARDIAN HATS: The Art of Millinery (1909) by Mme. Anna Ben-Yusuf

FEDERALIST AND REGENCY COSTUME: 1790-1819

THE GREAT WAR: Styles and Patterns of the 1910s

THE HANDBOOK OF PRACTICAL CUTTING on the Centre Point System (1866)
by Louis Devere

THE LADIES SELF-INSTRUCTOR in Millinery & Mantua Making, Embroidery & Applique (1853)

THE LADIES HANDBOOK of Fancy & Ornamental Work by Florence Hartley

LATE GEORGIAN COSTUME: The Tailor's Friendly Instructor (1822) by J. Wyatt
and THE ART OF TYING THE CRAVAT (1828) by H. LeBlanc

LATE VICTORIAN WOMEN'S TAILORING by T. H. Holding

REGENCY ETIQUETTE: The Mirror of Graces by A Lady of Distinction

SHIRTS AND MEN'S HABERDASHERY 1840s-1920s by R. L. Shep and Gail Cariou

TAILORING OF THE BELLE EPOQUE: Vincent's Systems of Cutting All Kinds of
Tailor-Made Garments (1903) by W. D. F. Vincent

VICTORIAN NEEDLE-CRAFT: Artistic & Practical (1889)

WOMEN'S FASHIONS 1877-1885: The Complete Dress & Cloak Cutter
by Charles Hecklinger

For more information and prices write to:

Fred Struthers, distributor
R.L. Shep Publications
Box 2706
Fort Bragg, CA 95437 USA   fsbks@mcn.org   www.rlshep.com